Metalworking 101 for Beaders

Metalworking 101 for Beaders

CREATE CUSTOM FINDINGS, PENDANTS & PROJECTS

Candie Cooper

LARK BOOKS

A Division of Sterling Publishing Co., Inc.
New York / London

EDITOR
Linda Kopp

ART DIRECTOR
Kathleen Holmes

ART PRODUCTION
Carol Morse

EDITORIAL ASSISTANCE
Amanda Carestio

PROJECT ILLUSTRATIONS
Candie Cooper

TEMPLATES
Orrin Lundgren

PHOTOGRAPHER
Lynne Harty

COVER DESIGNER
Chris Bryant

I'm dedicating this book
to my parents,
Tony and Jeanie Cooper,
who have held my hand
from the time I was born
to today.
I love you both.

Library of Congress Cataloging-in-Publication Data

Cooper, Candie, 1979-
    Metalworking 101 for beaders : create custom findings, pendants & projects /
Candie Cooper. —1st ed.
        p.   cm.
    Includes index.
    ISBN 978-1-60059-332-1 (pb-pbk. : alk. paper)
    1. Jewelry making.   2. Metal-work.   3. Beads.   I. Title.
TT212.C66 2009
739.27--dc22

                                                                    2009001435

10 9 8 7 6 5 4 3 2

Published by Lark Books, A Division of Sterling Publishing Co., Inc.
387 Park Avenue South, New York, NY 10016

Text and Illustrations © 2009, Candie Cooper
Photography © 2009, Lark Books, a Division of Sterling Publishing Co., Inc.
Author photograph Susan Stewart

Distributed in Canada by Sterling Publishing,
c/o Canadian Manda Group, 165 Dufferin Street
Toronto, Ontario, Canada M6K 3H6

Distributed in the United Kingdom by GMC Distribution Services,
Castle Place, 166 High Street, Lewes, East Sussex, England BN7 1XU

Distributed in Australia by Capricorn Link (Australia) Pty Ltd.,
P.O. Box 704, Windsor, NSW 2756 Australia

If you have questions or comments about this book, please contact:
Lark Books
67 Broadway
Asheville, NC 28801
828-253-0467

Manufactured in China

ISBN 13: 978-1-60059-332-1

For information about custom editions, special sales, premium and corporate purchases, please
contact Sterling Special Sales Department at 800-805-5489 or specialsales@sterlingpub.com.

contents

introduction

FINDINGS—THE LITTLE MECHANISMS that make our beaded creations come to life. They're so important to a jewelry piece, like a frame is to a painting. Findings perform a function, but they also enhance and beautify the overall work. Of course, you can purchase findings readymade, so why make your own? Well, I'm a firm believer in findings being as unique as the work they adorn. And if you're like me, you've got an awesome bead stash you're dying to use, but you might not be able to buy the perfect findings to go with each bead. *Metalworking 101 for Beaders* will show you how to make your own findings that match or complement the patterns and shapes of your beads. From bead caps to clasps, you can frame your beads perfectly!

You can make findings from just about any material; in this book I'll show you how to make them from copper, brass, and sterling. We'll explore making headpins, toggle clasps, hooks and eyes, pendants, rings, ear wires, hoops and more. You'll learn what materials to buy, what tools to use for removing sharp corners, and how to give your pieces an antiqued look.

Are you a little nervous about metalworking? Let me assure you, I was, too. I'll never forget the day, as a student back in Metalworking 101, I learned how to use a torch to anneal and solder. Now I teach workshops, and I often pass around the first pair of earrings I ever

made, wonky loops and all. They're not perfect by any means, but I was extremely proud, and my students see that practice does make perfect—and that anyone can do this. I'll teach you how to make metal soft and workable and how to make it sturdy, how to saw it, shape it, wrap it, and solder it. I'll show you tricks for texturing metal and how to color it to enhance those textures. The materials you'll need and techniques you'll use are all shown. Then it's on to the projects where you can apply what you've learned to make everything from your own simple ear wires to more complex projects like a tubing necklace.

Sprinkled throughout the projects you'll see little "From My Sketchpad" sections. These are additional ideas I had for variations on the pieces I made. I'm sure you'll have many of your own—tailor-made to suit your favorite beads. One thing is for sure, I think you'll find that "I made it myself" will take on a whole new meaning.

Metals

Manipulating metal—whether it's wire, sheet, or tube—is the heart of this book and will allow you to create impress-your-friends-and-family clasps, pendants, beads, and ear wires. Purchasing metal comes with all sorts of options including various thicknesses or gauges, hardness, and quantity. The thickness you use depends on what you intend to use it for—for example, earring parts don't need to be as thick as the base for a pendant. You'll also notice that when you sand a piece, you'll loose thickness, so take that into consideration before you dig into a project.

The hardness is specified with the terms "dead soft" or "half-hard." In layman's terms, dead-soft translates to more easily formed and manipulated. Half-hard has some resistance and holds its shape when formed. Most of the projects in this book use 18- to 22-gauge metal.

Sheet

The metals used for the projects in this book range from non-precious metals like copper and brass to precious metal sterling silver. I even used a bit of printed tin. Excluding the printed tin, any of these metals can be soldered together.

From vintage tin cans to precious gold, **sheet metal** makes the base of your findings and pieces. Be it rustic copper or polished silver, the metal you choose for your project will add a different flare or edge to your work. Raw material comes in flat sheets and wire starting at .15 mm thick and increasing to 2.60 mm thick, and these days you can even purchase it pre-textured!

A very soft metal, **copper** is a great practice material in that it's inexpensive and easy to work with. Also, the pinkish orange color of the metal makes it fun to mix with other metals. You can buy it in all gauges and wire shapes, including half-round and square.

Yellow in color, **brass** is an alloy comprised of 85 percent copper and 15 percent zinc. Also inexpensive compared to silver, it comes in sheets with a variety of gauges and round wire.

Sterling silver is an alloy or mixture of metal with 92.5 percent being silver and the other mostly copper. It's a very strong metal, which makes it the preferred metal to construct jewelry. You can reticulate sterling (a heating process that produces a ridged or rippled effect on the metal's surface, see page 26) because of its metal properties.

sheet

Fine silver is 99.9 percent pure silver and looks like a very bright white metal. Pure silver is typically too soft to use for large pieces in that it's not as durable as sterling, but because of its purity and melting temperature, it's great for fusing. Fine silver doesn't tarnish as quickly as sterling, and when it does, it looks more brass colored than black; this is helpful when the tags on your wire spools have fallen off and you need to figure out the difference between 18-gauge fine silver wire and 18-gauge sterling. The same principle applies for identifying sterling versus fine silver sheet metal.

Ordering Sterling Silver

Sterling sheet and wire are sold by the ounce based on the market price for silver that day. Most times, companies require you to order a minimum of ½ ounce (14 g). Depending on what size silver sheet you want, there can also be small cutting fees. When preparing your sheet order, one dimension of the silver must be 6 inches (15.2 cm) wide, but the other can be as long as 36 inches (91.4 cm).

It's worth keeping all your fine bits of silver scrap because you can sell it back to a company that has a reclaiming service for a percentage of the market price. Check with your jewelry supply company to see if they offer this service.

Wire

Just like sheet metal, wire comes in all metals, sizes, shapes, hardnesses, and even patterns. Again, what you're making determines what to purchase. There are colored craft wires, which cannot be heated. For a gold wire, try what's called gold-filled wire. Copper, brass, and sterling silver wire can be soldered and riveted. If you plan on fusing silver links for a chain, you need dead-soft fine silver wire. It's easily formed around a mandrel, and the ends melt together due to its purity. Dead-soft wire is also best if you want to wrap it around objects like beach glass or the tops of beads. If you want to make ear wires or head pins, buy half-hard sterling wire—it holds its shape. The scale of the object against the wire will help to determine what gauge wire you need for your project. In all cases, the smaller the gauge number, the thicker the wire.

You can use the **beading wire** you probably already have on hand for the projects in this book. The wire I use most often is a nylon coated, 49 strand, .018 diameter. There are also nice colored beading wires available.

MEASURE UP

The Brown & Sharpe System (B&S) is a standard way to measure the thickness of metal. A **gauge plate** is a tool in the shape of a disc with various sized notches going around it indicating thickness in gauge and thousandths of an inch. To use it, just slide your metal or wire into a notch where the fit is snug but not forced.

gauge plate

wire

Tubing

Tubing has many uses from making beads to rivets. If you look through a jewelry-making catalog, you'll see sterling tubing is available in square and round shapes and with thick and thin walls. Brass and copper tubing in various shapes can be purchased at smaller hardware stores (usually near the plumbing area).

tubing

BEADS, GLORIOUS BEADS

I've never met a bead I didn't like—from expensive to costing nearly nothing. The creatively outrageous and remarkable art beads available from indie bead makers are the perfect reason to make your own custom findings. For one, they add a truly unique flare to your work, and two, you are supporting an artist making their living through art. Bead shops, online auction/craft sites, catalog companies, flea markets with bags of junk jewelry, beading conventions, and trade shows are all great places to find super beads. My advice is to buy what you like, and don't feel like you have to use it tomorrow—it'll keep just fine in your stash until the right piece of jewelry presents itself.

Tools & Materials

If you've traveled this far in your jewelry-making adventure, you most likely know your stuff when it comes to beads. So let's skip the small talk and jump right into which tools and metals are uber-useful for making unique metal findings that'll add a WoW! factor to your jewelry creations.

Essential Tools

There are a few crucial tools when it comes to making jewelry: a jeweler's saw, a flexible shaft, and a bench pin. These can be purchased from a special jewelry supply catalog or online company.

When you go to purchase a **jeweler's saw**, you'll see that there are many saw frame options. I recommend the German jeweler's saw frame with a 4-inch (10.2 cm) throat depth (the throat depth determines how big a piece of metal you can move around). Since the projects in this book are small, this manageable frame works great, and it has a comfy grip.

jeweler's saw

Even more overwhelming is the choice of **saw blades** available for purchase. You'll want to buy blades based on what gauge metal you're sawing or how big you want your sawed lines to be if you're using them as a decorative element. The overall gist with blades is the more teeth a blade has per inch (cm), the finer the cut. Almost any jewelry supply catalog will contain a chart with specs for the different blade sizes—starting at an 8/0, which is .0063 inches (.16 mm) thick, and moving up to a size 8, which is .0197 inches (.5 mm) thick. I recommend a 1/0 blade simply because it's a great all-purpose blade for the gauges of metal used in this book. I've also had luck using that size for sawing thin plastic, dominos, and twigs. Lastly, blades come in different qualities. I love to pinch pennies but not when it comes to saw blades,

saw blades

so I go for the ones made in Germany. Quality blades are sharper and more flexible, which equals smoother sawing and less breaking. But I don't want to lead you to believe they're magically unbreakable! If you are a first timer, you will break blades regardless of quality.

SMOOTH THE WAY

You'll need a small cube of **beeswax** or other commercial lubricant for saw blades. The lubricant makes it easier for your saw blade to move through the material you're sawing. And trust me: you'll know when you've forgotten to apply it because you'll notice you're working three times as hard.

beeswax

- Jeweler's saw & blades
- Flexible shaft
- Bench pin
- Center punch & plastic mallet
- Chasing hammer
- Steel bench block
- Plier set (round nose, chain nose, flat nose, wire cutters)
- Liver of sulphur
- Pumice
- Sandpaper
- Files (hand and needle)
- Brass brush

Also called a "flex" shaft, the **flexible shaft tool** is one of the most versatile and beneficial tools to have on your workbench. With a large selection of attachment pieces, there are a multitude of ways you can use it, including sanding and finishing work, drilling holes, texturing metal—and all very quickly at that! You control the motor speed—and how fast the tool turns—using a foot pedal that is connected to the motor. Flex shafts come in a wide range of models, which leads to a wide range of prices. I started with a small, inexpensive handheld drilling tool and then worked my way up to a flexible shaft. You'll find there are several different hand-piece options for a flexible shaft, but the one I recommend has a chuck with a key that opens and closes the jaws on the hand-piece. It's compatible with different-size mandrels and tools. To keep your flex shaft in tip-top shape and give it a long life, follow the manufacturer's advice on maintenance. It's also good to buy or make a stand with pipe fittings that connects to your bench for the flex shaft motor to hang from. This keeps the actual flexible shaft in position so it doesn't get kinked, causing damage over time.

In order to support the metal you're sawing or filing, you'll need a **bench pin**. A bench pin clamps onto your worktable. Before making a purchase, the first thing to check is your table's thickness against how wide the bench pin's clamp opens. You'll see in the photo that my bench pin already has the "V" slot cut into it, but most bench pins don't come this way. This is so you can cut the "V" to suit your own personal preference. You can either cut a "V" using a slightly heavier-duty saw, or just opt to purchase a bench pin with a slot already cut into it. The bench pins with precut "V" slots tend to be a nice economical option.

Besides the "gotta have" tools listed above, you'll want to have a base set of secondary tools described in the next section; you'll find yourself reaching for them again and again. Consider the list at your left to be your basic Toolbox, and keep these items handy by your workbench. Happily, I think you'll find most of them to be fairly inexpensive.

bench pin

flexible shaft

AN ACCESSORY FOR EVERY NEED

For every task in making metal jewelry components, you can bet there's probably a flex shaft accessory tool that's perfect for the job. Just slip the attachment in the flex shaft. Examples include drill bits, cup burs, various abrasive wheels, mandrels, polishing wheels, heatless grinding wheels, and many, many more.

flex shaft attachment tools

Marking Tools

Just as a tailor needs his chalk, we need our marking tools for metal. You'll find there are different ones depending on the task.

A **center punch** is a piece of steel with a pointed end. It's used to make a small divot in the metal, marking the spot to be drilled and helping to keep your drill bit on target so it doesn't wander. The punch also creates a great decorative "dot" texture.

They don't call sterling silver "*precious* metal" for nothing. So before you start doing any metal cutting, you'll want to first transfer your design onto the metal's surface, and you can do that in a variety of ways. The first is with a fine-tip **permanent marker**. This is a very quick solution and should only be used for simple designs because it'll rub off with handling. Markers are also great for marking hole placement.

Another way to mark is with a **scribe**. Using the scribe like you would a pencil, you scratch lines into the metal around the outline of your pattern. While the lines are slightly difficult to see, they don't rub away. Lastly, a design drawn out or copied onto paper can be dry-mounted to the metal with rubber cement.

Remember using a compass in geometry class to draw precise circles? Well, a **divider** is used to perform the same function except on metal, not paper, and instead of a point and a pencil on the ends, the divider has two scribes. You can also use the edge of the metal as a guide and scribe an equal width strip of metal.

Forming Tools

Curves, twirls, and depth can be added to your metal pieces using forming tools. There's a vast assortment of special tools made for forming. At first glance, you may notice a hefty price tag for some of them, but I've found you can add a lot of zip to your pieces for a minimal cost if you use your jeweler's pliers and a simple hardwood-doming block.

Most beaders already have a **jeweler's plier set** (pliers clockwise from top: plastic-coated flat-nose, crimping, round-nose, wire cutters, chain-nose, snips), and you will most definitely put your wire cutters, and round-, flat-, and chain-nose pliers to good use making the findings in this book. It's beneficial to add a set of flat-nose pliers to your set if you haven't already. Flat-nose pliers work well for making 90° bends in wire and flattening small pieces of sheet metal.

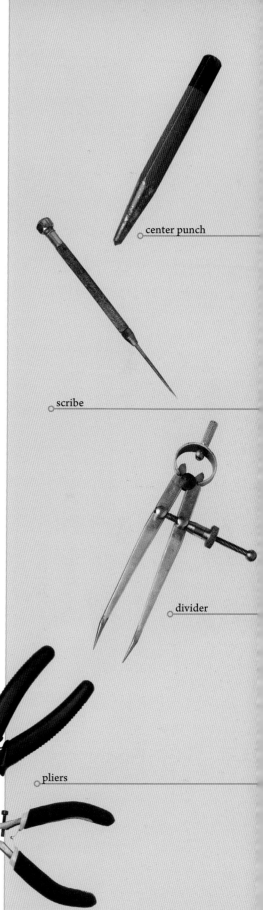

center punch

scribe

divider

pliers

13

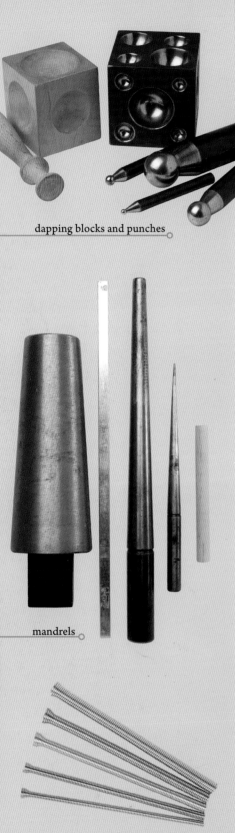

dapping blocks and punches

mandrels

tubing benders

A **dapping (or doming) block** has several half-sphere cavities in it and is used with a rounded punch—a tool that looks like steel shaft with a ball at the end. Punches make it easy to dome smaller-sized pieces of metal. These sets come in a range of prices depending on what material they're made of—steel or hardwood. For projects like bead caps, I prefer the steel block with deeper cavities. For more delicate doming, such as what is used to make the Gingko Necklace (page 74) or Geometric Brooches (page 98), I use a simple, inexpensive hardwood dapping block with shallow cavities.

Mandrels are smooth pieces of steel in various shapes and sizes used for shaping and forming (mandrels from left: bracelet, square tool stock, round ring, bezel, dowel rod). When placed in a vise, they make wonderful supports for hammering or texturing on because they're shaped exactly for the piece of jewelry you're making. Obviously a dowel rod is better used as a form for wrapping around rather than hammering on, but it is gentle on the pocket book! The three mandrels used in this book are ring, round bezel, and oval bracelet. The two that I use the most often are the round bezel for making ear wires and the ring for wrapping around large rings of metal. Mandrels come in round bracelet, neck forms, and various ring shapes. You'll find that which mandrels you purchase depends on what type of jewelry you like to make.

To bend sterling silver tubing like I did for the Charmed Tubing Necklace (page 80), you'll need to reach for your trusty **tubing bender**. A tubing bender consists of a coil of steel; when you slide a piece of tubing into the coil it spreads out the stress, allowing you to make a nice arch in the tubing. Without the steel coil, the tube will crease like a bent soda straw. I purchased my set from a large hardware supply store online.

Hammers

There are a ton of **hammers** made for metalworking—and they're made out of all sorts of materials (hammers from left: chasing, riveting, rawhide, claw, dead blow mallet). In an effort to keep the hammer topic brief, I'll cover only the ones used in this book.

When I say "hammer," likely the vision that pops into your mind is the traditional **claw hammer** that's probably in your utility drawer or out in your garage. You'll use this hammer for striking the ends of design or letter punches.

While the claw hammer serves well for many handyman jobs and has a place in this book,

hammers

the hammer I use most often in my pieces is the **chasing hammer**. It's great for texturing balled up wires or surfaces like the Geometric Silver Brooch (page 99) and for flattening rings, ear wires, and more. I also like the effect the chasing hammer produces on rivets; it leaves the rivet more rounded and textured versus nailhead-like—the result you get when using the riveting hammer.

As its name suggests, the **riveting hammer** is the appropriate hammer for riveting, but it also works well for texturing lines in metal, which is what I used it for in this book.

The heads of **rawhide and plastic mallets** are made of softer materials than their hammer counterparts, making them ideal tools for flattening metal while not damaging it. Heavier rawhide mallets are also gentle on your forming tools (i.e., dapping punch or center punch) because they won't mar the end of the punch, keeping it in good condition for years to come.

Flattening large pieces of metal calls for the heavyweight **dead-blow mallet**. The head of this ominously named mallet is filled with sand or shot, so that when you hit a surface the head lands with a solid "thump" and doesn't bounce back much. You can buy dead-blow mallets at your local hardware store.

Smoothing Tools

These days, there are lots of wonderful gizmos and gadgets that assist in removing burs, sharp corners, and edges from sawed metal pieces. It's important to have these tools on hand in order to create comfortable and safe components—or buy a lot of band-aids!

Files

Sometimes a deburring situation calls for some good old elbow grease. That's where **files** come in. They're used to remove small amounts of metal at a time, especially teeth marks after sawing. Files look like pieces of steel in different shapes (depending on the job) and come in different coarsenesses. Not just for smoothing, files also come in handy for texturing surfaces. It's worth mentioning that files don't normally come with handles because of individual grip preference and ergonomics. Instead, you purchase the type of handle you want separately and then connect it to the tang (the pointed end of the file), following the manufacturer's instructions.

In a jewelry supply catalog, you'll see numbers that indicate a file's coarseness (#8 fine down to #00 very coarse). If you buy only two files for your jewelry toolbox, the first should be an 8-inch-long (20.3 cm) **#2 flat hand file**. You'll find it useful for gradually removing metal from flat edges and surfaces. Another handy file to have is also 8 inches (20.3 cm) in length—the **#2 half-round ring hand file**, which does a fine job filing flat or curved surfaces. If you plan on creating fine pierced designs like the bamboo shoots seen on the Bamboo Bail (page 40) or the fin accents on Goldfish in Blue (page 77), you'll want to purchase a **needle file set**.

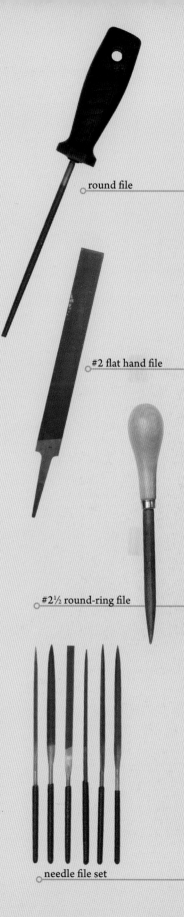

round file

#2 flat hand file

#2½ round-ring file

needle file set

file-cleaning brush

As you would suspect, needle files are very fine and are made specifically for filing in tight spaces. They normally come in sets containing six files, most often including a half-round, square, round, barrette, three-square, and equaling file. Lastly, for best results, you need to keep all those files clean of any metal bits, so have a **file cleaning brush** close by.

Abrasives

When it comes to removing scratches from your metal pieces, wet/dry abrasive paper is what to use. You can find it in your local hardware store or jewelry-making supply company. It comes in 9 x 11-inch (22.9 x 27.9 cm) sheets in a range of durable silicon carbide abrasives, with 150 grit being very rough to 1500 being very smooth. The projects in this book use 220-, 320-, 400-, and 600-grit papers.

To quickly sand two edges of a surface flush, you'll want to use **snap-on sanding discs**. They're ⅞-inch (2.2 cm) sandpaper-covered discs that come in a variety of grits and are quite flexible, making them perfect for working edges as well as surfaces. Don't forget to purchase the special mandrel that the discs snap onto.

snap-on sanding discs

Another all-around fabulous abrasive attachment is a **radial bristle disc**. It has skinny, rubberlike abrasive "fingers" with a flexible design that allows it to squeeze into cracks and crevices, finishing those hard-to-reach spots. They range in colors, with each color indicating a different grit. You'll find yourself reaching for this little gem time and time again. Don't forget to buy a screw mandrel to hold the disc so it can be used in a flexible shaft.

radial bristle discs

For obvious reasons, it's essential to get the inside and edges of ring shanks and the ends of ear wires as smooth as glass. A **slotted mandrel** wrapped with sandpaper is just the tool for a ring shank because you can go over the contours easily. A cup burr perfectly and quickly rounds the end of a wire—great when making earrings. You can purchase a cup burr that fits into a flexible shaft, or one with a handle and turn it by hand.

SCRIMPING VS CRIMPING

Some of the projects' beadwork will be finished with crimp beads, so you'll need a pair of crimping pliers to securely close the beads. I'm sure many of you are already familiar with crimping pliers and already have a pair ready to wield. Possibly less familiar are scrimps, which are small beads with screws that loosen and tighten to secure the wire inside them. A miniature screwdriver will come with your scrimps so you can easily secure the screw inside. I find that sometimes I choose a scrimp over a crimp bead because they don't accidently crack like a crimp bead or tube can, and I can easily adjust the length before cutting the wire.

scrimp

slotted mandrels

Assembly Tools

There are many forms of assembly that come with making your own components and jewelry. You'll use your beadwork knowledge to connect beads to the findings as well as learning about hot and cold connections. Cold connections, such as riveting, are used for metals where the surface will be damaged by heat. They can also be used for decorative elements. Hot connections, like soldering, are very sturdy and fairly quick. Presented here are a few tools and items you'll use in assembling your findings and gems.

Soldering Tools

Adding soldering to your jewelry-making repertoire opens many creative doors, but it also adds a new set of needs. You have to take into consideration your work area and add a few more materials to your workbench, including a torch, flux, solder, and a special work surface. For this book, I opted to solder all the projects with a **small pencil torch** that runs on propane. It's wonderful in that it's quite inexpensive (you can easily drop a bundle for a torch), and it doesn't take up much space. This particular torch connects to the small propane canisters many folks use with camping stoves and lanterns. The downside to this torch is that you can't heat up larger-sized pieces very easily with it.

Your pencil torch won't be a load of use to you without **solder**. Silver solder is what flows between two pieces of metal and, after cooling, makes a permanent bond. It can be bought in sheets which can be cut with shears, or in wire form, which you snip into very tiny chips with wire cutters. I still use the old-school wire solder and sheet solder, but you can now purchase precut chips of solder. They get the job done that much quicker.

Silver solder has five different melting points, allowing you to do multiple soldering operations on the same piece without the connections coming apart each time you heat it. The names of these five solders and their melting points are:

"IT" 1490°F (810°C)

"Hard" 1425°F (773°C)

"Medium" 1390°F (754°C)

"Easy" 1325°F (718°C)

"Extra Easy" 1270°F (688°C)

sheet solder

third hand tool

pencil torch

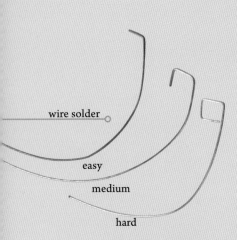

wire solder

easy

medium

hard

tweezers

Sheet solder comes stamped with its grade. You can see in the photo that wire solder can be easily marked with 90° bends—one bend for "easy," two for "medium," and three for "hard." Because the projects in this book only have one-to-three step soldering options per piece, this book uses Extra Easy through Medium silver solders. As your metal pieces grow in complexity, Hard and IT will be more useful.

Where there's solder, there needs to be **paste flux**. Paste flux is simply what keeps your metal from oxidizing or getting dirty when bringing the piece up to soldering temperature with the torch. I like to use white paste flux because you can use it with silver, copper, and brass, and it can withstand a lot of heating. Flux can be purchased from a jewelry supply company; you'll need a small paintbrush to apply it to your metal.

When working with tools that generate high temperatures or have an open flame like a pencil torch, you'll want to protect your workbench with a **high heat block** made of heat-reflective material. One such block is a **honeycomb or plain ceramic block**, or you could try a **soldering pad** made of a non-asbestos material that is very light. A neat feature of the honeycomb design is that you can use pins to keep your work in place when you solder, and it spreads out the heat evenly. The soldering pad is nice because it comes in a range of sizes, and you can drill holes in it or modify it to fit your needs. I like to have one large base block and then several smaller pieces of heat block to prop my work on.

In some instances you'll find yourself needing to place chips of solder onto metal or to pick up hot pieces of metal so you can quench them in cool water. A pair of **stainless steel tweezers** is what you want (tweezers from left: fine tip stainless, copper, stainless steel). Admittedly, I've used my brow-tweezing ones in a pinch. However, the type you want to use has very fine tips, enabling precision work.

KEEPING IT CLEAN

Metal looks a little charred after soldering, sporting a flakey black surface from the oxidation. You can remove that by using a mild sulphuric acid bath called **pickle**. Copper or bamboo tongs must be used in the acid because of the chemical reaction between steel and the acid.

After soldering and pickling, clean your piece with some **pumice powder**. Pumice powder grit comes in medium, fine, and flour grit. For this final cleaning step, you'll want to use fine. Just moisten your fingers with water, dip the tips into the powder, and rub them over the metal until there's no residue and the water sheets evenly on the metal. You can use an old toothbrush to clean tight areas.

Texturing & Finishing

As mentioned in the section on chasing and riveting hammers, you can create some great textures, but you'll need a hard surface that's conducive to the process; meet the **bench block**. A bench block is made of hardened steel and is ideal for pounding textures, flattening wire, riveting, and work-hardening metal.

I admit it; I *love* **liver of sulphur**. It's an easy-to-use chemical that antiques copper, brass, and silver surfaces. As you work through the project pieces, you'll notice that I toss many of my jewelry components into a liver of sulphur bath to knock off the high shine. After polishing, the recessed areas remain darker, thus highlighting the detail work. Liver of sulphur is purely a personal preference choice.

I feel a **brass brush** is indispensible, and I use it on the finishes of most of my pieces. This tool is just what it sounds like—a brush with soft brass bristles. Use it along with a couple of drops of dishwashing soap and water to add a gentle shine to your metal or to burnish over a liver of sulphur patina.

If you want a little more shine after brass brushing your piece, try going over it with a **polishing cloth**. Polishing cloths are made of a soft material, and they already have a polishing compound in them so you don't need to apply any creams or cleaning solutions. They clean and shine any metal and will not remove the liver of sulphur patina. The harder you work, the shinier your metal will be.

liver of sulphur

Nice-to-Have Tools

As you learn the ways of working with metal, you will discover lots of gadgety-whatcha-macall-its to fall in love with for a variety of reasons including ease, efficiency, and safety. Until you develop your own list of favs, below are tools I've found to be most useful.

Like me, I'd be willing to bet that there's been a time or two when you've wished for an extra hand. Wish granted! While not a helping hand for, say, doing the dishes, the aptly named **third hand base** (with cross-lock tweezers) is used for holding pieces in precarious positions so you can safely solder them together. For example, when you want to solder a jump ring to a domed disc, let the third hand help you out.

Without a doubt, tumblers are a bit pricey, but if you plan on making a lot of parts and pieces, a **tumbler** will save you hours in polishing time. Polishing using a tumbler instead of by hand is like the difference between washing clothes using a washing machine versus a washboard. Pop your pieces and some steel shot into a tumbler, and let it sand and polish the edges, as well as all those hard-to-reach areas. I recommend using stainless steel shot. You can opt for the cheaper steel shot, but it'll rust if you leave the water in the tumbler. It doesn't take too long to tumble a batch of pieces to a nice high shine. You can buy tumblers and steel shot from jewelry companies.

brass brush

Basic Metalworking Techniques

Now for the fun part—learning and trying some metalworking techniques. I remember when I first started working with tiny pieces of metal: there were definitely some frustrating times when I made mistakes and wasn't quite sure how to fix them—or even if they were fixable. It's important to allow yourself to make mistakes (you will learn a ton from them) and then keep on truckin'! As the old saying goes, practice makes perfect...

Marking

There are a couple of different ways to transfer a design to metal. If you have a template, you can use a **scribe** to trace your pattern onto the metal. I recommend this approach only for simple designs like circles or squares, because, depending on your lighting, the scribed lines are sometimes hard to see.

This next method is the one I use most often. Many times I'll draw my finding idea on paper to make a pattern, because then I can manipulate it to the exact size I want. If it's a design you plan to reuse, trace over any pencil lines with ink or make a photocopy. Paint a thin layer of rubber cement on both the backside of the design and the top of the metal, then let them dry. Gently place your pattern onto the metal and burnish so that it's secure.

Marking a line with a divider

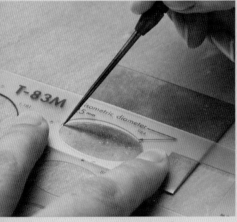
Using a template and scribe

Adhering a pattern to metal using rubber cement

Sawing

Before your first saw stroke, you need to clamp your bench pin to the table and put a saw blade into your saw frame. Saw blades come in little bundles of 12, wrapped with brass wire. Unwrap one end of the wire just enough so that you can slide a blade out. Note the teeth orientation on the blade—they should be pointing down. Now, holding your saw frame vertically by its handle, take a look and you'll notice three thumbscrews. We'll refer to the handle end as the "bottom" of the saw and the opposite metal end as the "top." Loosen the two thumbscrews at the top of the saw just enough so the blade sits down in the slot. No need to mess with the back third thumbscrew at this time. Slide the blade up into the slot so that the end of the blade goes all the way to the top. Check to make sure the blade is straight up and down and that the teeth are facing out and pointing down toward the bottom—like a pine tree—and tighten the screw. Note where the bottom of the saw blade ends in conjunction with the slot—it should be approximately one-third of the way down. If it's not, loosen that mysterious third screw and slide the top of the saw frame down or up a bit and then tighten.

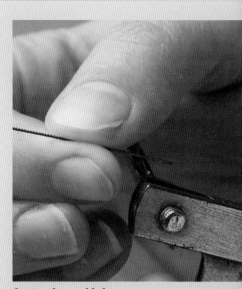

Seating the saw blade

If you push the top of the frame against the handle, you'll notice the frame has some spring to it. This is so you can add tension to the saw blade. Do this by placing the top of the frame into the "V" slot on your bench pin with the blade side facing up, and push in toward the bench pin so the end of the handle rests in your sternum so you're closing the frame up a little. Although it feels kind of strange, this position frees up your hands so you can hold the blade in place with one hand and tighten the last thumbscrew with the other. Check to make sure your saw blade has enough tension by plucking it. It should make more of a "ping" sound than a "thud." If it "thuds," loosen the bottom screw, reposition the frame between the bench pin and your sternum, and push in a little harder, retightening the screw.

Bench pin clamped to a work surface

Adding tension to the saw frame

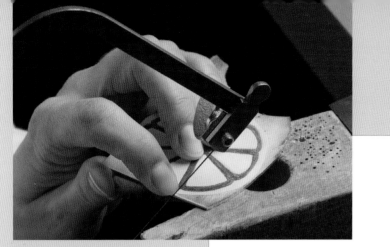

Begin sawing at a 45° angle

Gradually straighten the frame as you saw

Now you're just moments away from sawing! Add a tad of beeswax on the sides of the blade—it doesn't take much. This is a situation where you can have too much of a good thing and end up clogging the teeth of the blade.

Lay your piece of metal on the bench pin. Now a quick but important word about safety: I can't overemphasize the importance of keeping the fingers that hold the metal BEHIND the blade. Even though the blade appears to be thin, delicate, and harmless, it's sharp and can cut you faster than the blink of an eye. So when using your saw, make sure you're well rested and alert. Position your saw blade so the upper half of it is resting at the starting point of your design and the frame of the saw is at a 45° angle—so the top of the frame is closer to the metal. Place the nail of your index finger just next to the blade and gently move the saw up and then back down. Repeat gradually, straightening the saw frame to an upright position with each stroke. Saw just to the outside of your pattern line. Take care not to angle your saw from right to left, or you may end up removing more material than you planned.

With such a tiny blade, it's tempting to try turning it on a dime, but in most cases the blade will snap. If you've ever used a band saw, using a jeweler's saw is much the same in that you make turns slowly by sawing a few strokes almost in place, as you turn. This method will create a slightly rounded corner. For crisp corners, saw in from two different directions to get a perfect point.

To saw pieces of tubing, lay the piece on either end of your bench pin. Begin sawing as usual, except saw right into the wood. That way you can reuse the sliced area again and again whenever you saw tubing. If you have multiple pieces to cut, align the point to be sawed with the slit in the wood.

CUES FROM CANDIE

Sawing out shapes in the middle of a design is called **piercing**. If your design has inside details that need sawing out, I recommend doing those first so you can leave as much metal around the perimeter as possible. Be sure to read the drilling section on page 30, and then with the design facing up, thread the saw blade through the drilled hole and reattach the blade.

Smoothing

If you look at the sawed edges of your piece, you'll see there are vertical marks left from the sawing. Filing with a **hand file** will smooth away these teeth marks. Hold the metal on top of the bench pin so the cut edge is slightly hanging off one side of the pin. Like the saw blade, there are teeth on a file that do the cutting; if you look closely, you'll see the angled grooves. Before you begin, know that a file only cuts on the upstroke. It actually dulls the file's sharp teeth by dragging it back down. Begin filing with the top of the file down near the metal's edge and then push upward, keeping the file perpendicular to the metal's edge. When you get to the end, lift the file and start again with an upward stroke. For outside curves, use an upward sweeping motion around the outside. For interior curves, use a half-round file and the same sweeping action to help keep the rounded shape. The end result should be a clean, flat, ribbon-like edge.

Use **needle files** to go over every edge, removing the hand file teeth marks. They work exactly like their larger hand file kin, except they can fit into those pesky tight spots. You can use them to make inside corners crisper, and there's a shape for every crevice.

Run a file cleaning brush over the surface so the bristles run down in the grooves, pushing the metal out.

If you look closely at your metal, you'll probably see some scratches and feel some rough edges. Grab your **sandpaper** so we can clean things up! I generally start with the 220-grit sandpaper, but if my metal is really beat up (i.e., deep scratches), I start with the coarser 150. Lay your sheet of sandpaper on a clean, flat work surface. You might want to tape it down with masking tape so it doesn't slide around.

Filing an outside curve

Using a half-round file on an interior curve

A needle file can fit in small places

23

Vertical lines from sanding

Place your metal piece flat on the sandpaper and begin sliding it back and forth. Periodically turn the piece 180° in order to sand it evenly. After a few minutes of sanding you'll see vertical lines and, hopefully, all the scratches and nicks will have vanished. If you like this effect, you can leave the piece as is, but if you want a silky smooth surface, push on to 320 grit. Turn your piece 90° before you begin, and sand so that at first the lines from the sanding and the lines from the previous grit are crossing each other. Keep going until all you can see are the 320-grit lines. It's important not to move on to the next grit until all the lines from the previous grit are gone. Believe it or not, they'll show up on the final finish if you ignore them—take it from me, who's already tried it. Now move up to 400-grit paper, turn your piece 90°, and continue sanding. Finish up with 600 grit. Repeat for the backside.

One thing to watch out for when sanding is your metal's thickness. Sanding can thin edges quicker than you might think, especially if you don't rotate your piece 180° while sanding. I notice that sometimes I tip the piece ever so slightly forward while sliding it on the paper, resulting in one side that's thinner than the other; that's why it's important to turn your piece.

STICK TO IT

Texturing

There are endless ways to texture a piece of metal in any thickness. I'll tell you a few of my favorites, but I think you'll find that experimenting with scraps of copper and different texturing tools will lead to greatness, adding your own special touch to your creations.

Texturing is one of the last steps in the creation process. All filing, sanding, and, most of the time, drilling should be complete. The only time drilling should be done after texturing is when using rivets, or if the texturing process will misshape the hole—i.e. if you're using a hammer. Just as when you saw, support your work on a bench pin or benchblock. You can form textured pieces in the wood dapping block, or dome them first and then texture.

Get creative with your sanding and you'll be surprised at the textures you can produce. Once when I was in Germany, I saw a goldsmith texturing a ring shank with heavy grit sandpaper and small circular motions. Playing around with the concept, I found this finish looks best if you sand the piece to 600 and then go over it with 150-grit paper. Another idea to try is to apply a liver of sulphur patina first, brass brush, and then go over it with 150- or 220-grit sandpaper. It'll scratch away the patina, leaving contrasting colored hairlike lines (the bead caps in the Etruscan Earrings [page 84] have this treatment).

I don't know about you, but I find it very therapeutic to **hammer** on some metal. If you're opting for a hammered texture, supporting your work on something like a steel mandrel or bench block is essential to keeping the shape of your piece while you beat on it. Without support, the metal will take the shape of whatever's under it. One time I dented a wood table because I forgot to put the bench block under my metal! If you'd like, you can put a dish towel under your block to dull the hammering sound and help protect your work surface. A vise that clamps or bolts onto your workbench holds mandrels nicely so you can work on rings and things of that nature.

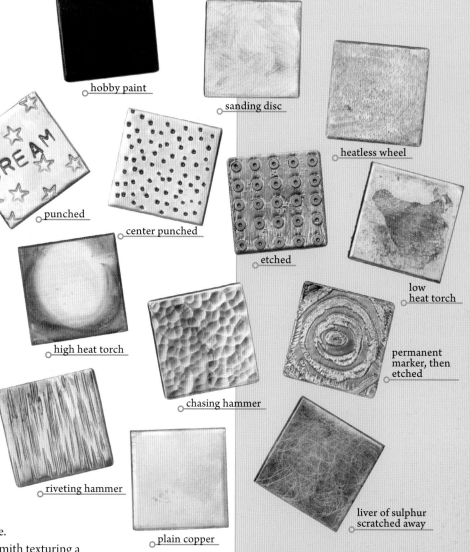

hobby paint

sanding disc

heatless wheel

punched

center punched

etched

low heat torch

high heat torch

chasing hammer

permanent marker, then etched

riveting hammer

plain copper

liver of sulphur scratched away

Texturing on a steel mandrel

Making a dot pattern with a center punch

You can create a lovely dot pattern with only your **center punch** and a mallet. The dot depths will vary depending on how hard you strike the end of the punch. Use a heavy claw hammer to strike the ends of **letter and design stamps**. Be sure you have the stamp in the right orientation. Support your work on a steel bench block to get the best results.

The attachments that are used with the **flexible shaft** are especially fun for experimentation with texture. Sanding discs and diamond burrs both create interesting effects. The heatless wheel tool, which is like a mini grinding wheel, creates another good finish, especially for rings, because scratches don't show up so easily.

Reticulation is a somewhat scientific process that uses heat along with sterling to create a surface with ripples and ridges. The Tassel Necklace on page 52 has reticulated bead caps. Fine silver will not work for this process, only sterling. You can even find a special alloy sold in jewelry supply companies that's intended for reticulation. There are a few downsides to reticulating silver. One is that the process has a mind of its own, making it pretty much impossible to control the results. Secondly, after the final heating, the metal can sometimes become brittle and crack during forming. Lastly, the porous surface is sometimes tricky to solder along using a lower melting temperature, so use medium or easy solder. But reticulated silver looks so intriguing, you'll wish every metal could do it!

If you want to give reticulation a shot, the first step is to lift the fine silver to the surface of the sterling silver sheet. Do this by placing your silver on a heat-safe pad and heating the silver to the annealing point (the silver will turn a dull red), then carefully quench it in pickle, and rinse. Repeat three or four more times—you'll see the bright white color of the fine silver present itself. Now your metal is ready. I like

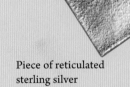

Piece of reticulated sterling silver

Various letter and design punches

to first heat the heat-safe pad up a little using a "fluffy" flame before I actually lay the metal down. Place the metal on your heated block and continue heating until the metal starts to melt, then slowly move your flame over the surface until it's all melted.

Etching allows you endless ways to embellish copper. To add additional interest, I etched the copper tube bails on the Charmed Tubing Necklace (page 80). When **etching copper**, I use **ferric chloride**. There are ways to etch sterling, but the chemical is extremely dangerous, so I stick to etching copper. You can sometimes buy ferric chloride or PCB etchant in electronics shops because it's used for printed circuit boards (PCB). I purchase my etchant online. As for the design, I use anything from rub-on decals or nail polish to special permanent markers (also sold online) to create a resist. Etchant solution will eat away anywhere on the metal where there's not a resist, including the edges. Pour the etching solution in a plastic or glass container until it measures 1½ to 2 inches (3.8 to 5 cm) deep. Cut a piece of tape long enough to allow each end to be attached to either side of your plastic container and to have enough slack that when you attach your copper pieces to the tape, they'll be soaking in the etchant. Stick your copper pieces to the tape, and rub the surfaces to make sure they're completely burnished down. Attach the tape to each side of the container, suspending your pieces facedown in the liquid. Leave them in the solution for approximately 30 minutes, agitating the solution from time to time. Check the pieces every 10 to 15 minutes until you've reached the desired etched depth. To remove the resist, rinse and scrub the pieces with water, pumice, and a toothbrush.

Making etching patterns using a marker and rub-on decals

Soaking copper pieces in etchant solution

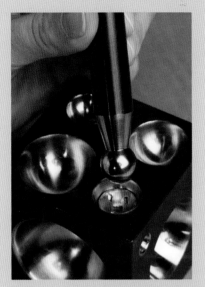
Doming a disc in a dapping block

Forming

Forming is simply giving shape to metal—be it wire made into a spiral or metal sheet shaped into a domed disc—and each metal has its own degree of malleability. For instance, you'll find that copper will stay malleable longer than sterling when forming. The pieces in this book require only simple forming, easily accomplished with pliers, mandrels, and dapping blocks. If you take a look around your house, you may find things that would be good for forming lying around the garage or in drawers.

FLEXIBILITY THROUGH ANNEALING

Have you ever bent a soft wire back and forth to the point that it broke? Well what happened was this: after all that bending, the wire became work-hardened. The process of annealing softens the metal by heating it with a torch to a specific temperature. This is useful because you can make metal softer so it's easier to form, and then strengthen it through work hardening. When you dome pieces such as discs when making bead caps, you'll find that by annealing the metal first, you can stretch and shape it much easier. Another time annealing is helpful is when you're making wire rivets. Annealing the wire makes it soft, so you can easily form rivet heads.

I first annealed the copper strips used in the Charmed Tubing Necklace (page 80) before trying to form them; otherwise it would have been really tricky to wrap the ends around so they met up nicely. It's worth mentioning that you may need to anneal the metal more than once while you're forming because forming work-hardens the metal. Simply heat the metal to the annealed point, pickle, and continue forming.

To anneal metal, first paint it with a layer of flux and then gently go over the metal with the torch flame, slowly letting the moisture burn away. When the flux is dry you can apply heat more directly. You'll know the metal is annealed when the white flux turns clear. Flux isn't required to anneal metal, but the glassy clear appearance of the flux is a helpful indicator for beginners. Another good indicator is the color that the metal changes to once annealed: low red for copper and medium red for sterling. Once you learn what to look for, you can skip fluxing the metal.

Doming

Dapping blocks with various cavity depths and punches will dome metal pieces. To form domed shapes you must first start with annealed or soft metal. Choose a cavity depth, place your metal over it, and strike the end of the punch with a mallet. Using a mallet with a plastic or rawhide head will help preserve the end of your punches. As you strike with the mallet, listen for the "ping"—this sound indicates that you've reached the bottom of the steel dapping block and can't go any deeper, but the sides of your piece can still be domed by rotating the disc in the cavity and continuing to punch. With each strike of the punch, the metal will harden a little more. If your piece is larger than the cavity, rotate the shape as you form, working all the angles. I especially like using my shallow cavity hardwood dapping block in these cases.

Bending

The easiest way to apply a slight arch to metal tubing is with **tubing or coil benders**. Tubing benders are sold in sets with varying sizes to allow you to bow ¼, ⅜, ½, and ⅝ inch (6 and 9.5 mm, and 1.3 and 1.6 cm) diameter tubing. Select a bender in which the tubing fits snugly, and then push the bender against a large bracelet mandrel, or around something similar, like a table leg.

Mandrels are useful when forming because they give you a solid form to wrap your metal around. You can use a plastic mallet, lay your metal piece over a mandrel, and tap it into shape or simply use your fingers to push the metal into shape—as I did with the Profusion Ring (page 59) ring band—to make a symmetrical curve. You can form a perfect ring by sliding your fused wire loop onto a mandrel and tapping it into shape with a plastic mallet. Square or oval-shaped mandrels are nice for making unique jump rings (you can spot some square jump rings on the Charmed Tubing Necklace on page 80).

Curving an over-size piece

tubing (or coil) benders

HANDS-FREE FORMING

Look at the jaw of your bench vise, and you may see a round slot with teeth. That's for holding round mandrels, allowing your hands to be free while you form. Depending on what's most comfortable for you, you can also hold the mandrel in your hands.

Arching tubing in a bender over a bracelet mandrel

Assembling

There are many options when it comes to putting all the pieces together. Ultimately, your design will decide what works and looks best. You may find that some things work like a charm, and that other projects need tweaking or modifying. Below you'll find key techniques you'll use when assembling your pieces.

Drilling

The key to drilling is careful planning. Mark the hole placement on your metal using a fine-tip permanent marker. Take care to note the size of the hole you want in conjunction with how close you put the hole to the edge of the metal. For smaller-sized drill bits, 1 mm is about the minimum distance I like to get from the edge. Lay your metal on a steel block. Position the tip of the center punch on top of the dot, and strike the end with a plastic or rawhide mallet. No need to whack it; just a light tap should make enough of a divot. You need a divot so when your drill bit meets the metal, it won't skid and slide all over the place. Set your metal piece on top of a scrap wood surface. Attach the appropriate bit to the flexible shaft tool, and begin drilling. No need to push; it should cut through the metal pretty easily. Drill bits create friction when drilling and thus heat up your metal, so it's best to drill a little, wait for the metal to cool, and start again. Drill bits become dull over time, which slows your cutting speed and creates more heat.

This next bit of information is important! When drilling larger-sized holes, start with a small-size drill bit and slowly increase the hole size using gradually larger bits; this is some "I learned it the hard way" advice. I initially thought I could save time by using a large-size bit, but instead found myself with a very hot piece of metal because the bit tried to shred its way through the metal. I had to start all over, wasting material and time.

Making a divot for drilling

Drilling holes to insert the saw blade

EQUIVALENCY CHART

B&S Gauge	Inches	Drill Size
5	$3/16$	15
6	$5/32$	20
8	$1/8$	30
11	$3/32$	43
14	$1/16$	51
18	$3/6$	55
20	$1/32$	65

This chart is a quick reference to the gauge of your metal, be it wire or sheet, with English thickness measurement and drill bit size. It's particularly useful when you want to make rivets because you can match the drill bit size to the gauge of wire you're using.

Connecting

In order to make jewelry we must make connections—using jump rings, solder, rivets, wrapped wire, and other methods. The following is merely a jumping-off point for the many techniques for making connections in your jewelry designs.

Rivets connect layers of materials together. Among your rivet choices are wire, tubing, and tiny nuts and bolts. Why rivet? Well, first off, because it looks cool! Secondly, you can use rivets for situations where soldering is not possible because of the materials you're connecting—such as printed tin, plastic rulers, or leather. But going back to the first point, rivets can be a purely decorative element, as in the Geometric Copper Brooch (page 98), or functional as well as decorative, as in the Paisley Interchangeable Bracelet (page 69). When planning a riveted design, remember that at least two rivets are needed in order for the piece on top not to spin. Any gauge wire can be used, from 20 gauge up to 12 gauge.

Before you begin the riveting process, anneal your wire or tubing and then clean it in a pickle solution. Using a drill bit that's the exact same diameter as the wire or tubing you're going to use as a rivet, drill a hole through the material you wish to rivet. The fit of the wire has to be snug or your rivet won't work. If you have multiple layers of metal or objects, center punch and drill all the holes in the top metal piece, then use masking tape to secure the two pieces together. There's no need to center punch the base metal piece because the top piece's holes will act as a guide. Drill the base metal holes one at a time, sliding a piece of wire through the two layers to lock them in place; this keeps them from shifting during the drilling and ensures that the holes in both pieces will line up when it's time to rivet.

riveted charms

ALL WOUND UP

I won't pretend like I handmake every single jump ring for my jewelry pieces. But there are certain situations when you need an odd size or you want to make a woven chain. There're many ways to make a jump ring but I'll show you two of the ways I make mine.

It all basically comes down to the jump ring's diameter. For smaller, precise jump rings, I use a jump ring maker tool. With it you can crank out a lot of rings quickly and easily. Secure the wire to the hole in the plexiglass, then twirl the plastic piece around, guiding the wire so it coils nicely on the mandrel. Another way is to wrap the wire around a dowel rod; this works well too—especially for larger rings. Regardless of which method you use, a wrapped half-inch length coil seems to be the most manageable to cut. When you're finished wrapping, secure the coil with a piece of masking tape. Slide the coil off the mandrel, and cut through it using sharp snips. Remove the tape and, if all went well, you should have a nice little pile of jump rings. Sometimes I file the ends of the ring so they meet up perfectly—especially if I plan to fuse the ends of the rings together.

Using a jump ring maker

Snipping through the coil

Surprisingly, not much wire needs to be sticking up on either side of your layers in order to create a rivet. For both wire and tubing, only half the diameter of the wire or tube is needed on each side. For example, if your tubing or wire is 1 mm in diameter, you need .5 mm sticking up on the top and .5 mm on the underside. Cut the wire so it's slightly longer, and file it down to the correct length with a needle file so the full diameter of the wire is showing.

To make a **wire rivet**, hold your metal piece just above the steel bench block, with the wire resting on the block, and gently (extra emphasis on gently) tap the top of the wire a few times with the angled end of a riveting hammer or the rounded end of a chasing hammer. Turn the piece over and repeat. Work both sides evenly, flipping the piece, until you have a nice "mushroom-like" cap on both sides of the metal. If you'd like the rivet to look flat like a nail head, use the flat side of a hammer.

When making a **tube rivet**, I use an oversized center punch placed in the center of the tubing opening, give a few taps with the mallet, and flip to the other side and repeat. Continue until both sides have rolled down evenly, and finish by tapping with a steel dapping punch or the round end of the chasing hammer.

Tubing comes in the same measurements as drill bits. Some of my favorite tube diameters are $\frac{3}{16}$, $\frac{5}{32}$, $\frac{1}{8}$, and $\frac{3}{32}$ inch (5, 4, 3, and 2.5 mm).

I find **mini nuts and bolts** addictive! They're a little tricky because of their size but so wonderfully instant. But don't run to your local hardware store looking for these little gems; you'll find them at special jewelry supply companies online. Be sure to purchase a diminutive wrench set, too. It's a must when working with these tiny pieces. To use, drill a hole as you would for riveting with wire. From the back, thread the bolt through all the layers, then connect a mini washer and a nut. Cut the excess bolt away just above the nut, leaving just enough for a rivet. File so the bolt is a perfect circle, and tap the end with a chasing hammer. This makes it so the bolt can't accidentally unscrew and come apart.

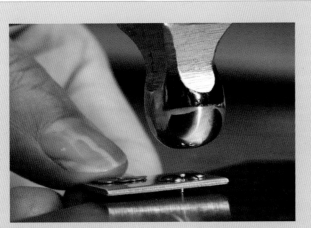

Beginning a wire rivet

Using a center punch on a tube rivet

Finishing a tube rivet with a dapping punch

Mini nuts and bolts

Soldering

When I was first learning to use a **torch**, I looked at it like it was a fire-breathing beast. It was absolutely intimidating, but after turning it on and off a few times, my anxiety lessoned. Being able to use a torch busts down many doors when it comes to making jewelry. The manufacturer's instructions are the best place to start to learn how to operate your particular torch. Here are four general rules of safety that should be followed:

- Have some sort of exhaust in place for the fumes from your torch.
- Always turn your torch off at the tank.
- Bleed the lines by turning on the gas at the torch head and letting the gas in the line escape, then turn the torch off at the head.
- Keep your torch in a safe area away from children.

Soldering opens up many creative possibilities. From placing an ear post on a pierced piece of metal to making a simple pinback, soldering makes it that much easier to make custom-designed pieces. The projects in this book use medium down to extra easy solder. Note that by adjusting a knob on your torch, you can alter the intensity of the flame from "fluffy" to a sharp point.

Before you begin to solder, it's good to know four important "musts." 1) The pieces to be joined must fit together well, 2) they must be clean, 3) always use flux, and 4) both pieces need to be at the same temperature at the same time so the solder will flow between them.

1. When I say the pieces must have a good fit, I mean the contact surface areas on both pieces should be maximized. For example, wire that's been filed and sanded to the full diameter will solder better to a sheet than one that has a pinched-looking end after being cut. If you're soldering a piece of tubing for a bail (as seen in the Serene Cross necklace on page 100), there can be no space between the cross and tubing. If there's a gap, the solder won't flow. Countless times I've wished that solder could be like putty, but it's not. Tip: File a flat spot on jump rings and tubing to prevent the pieces from rolling away while you're soldering them, and to create more surface area for the connection.

2. Pickle, pumice and clean all the pieces before soldering. If there's any sort of oxidation from a previous soldering operation in the area where you want solder to flow, it won't work. Use a toothbrush and pumice to get in the cracks and crevices, and clean, clean, clean.

3. Flux all the pieces where you want them to join.

4. If your piece has more than one area to be soldered, deciding which piece you solder first depends on how many connections need to be made overall and how close the pieces to be soldered are to each other. For example, if pieces to be soldered are near one another, the initial soldered piece will become undone with the second soldering, unless a solder with a higher melting point is used first. So let's say you have three areas to be soldered. First, start with the solder that has a higher temperature melting point—like hard or medium. For the next solder, use medium or easy, and then easy or extra easy for the last.

HEAT PROTECTION

Remember that bit about all your pieces must be clean in order for solder to flow? Well, if you've already soldered a piece, and you don't want to chance it coming apart while you're soldering the next piece, place a line of correction fluid on either side of the seam and let it dry. It's not invincible to heat, but it'll last for a pretty lengthy time.

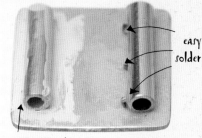

easy solder

soldered with medium solder

Let's take for example the Fanciful Feathered Friends projects; the birds' beaks on the front side of the metal and the pin findings on the back both needed to be soldered. Because of their close proximity to each other, either one could come apart as you are soldering the opposite. In order to prevent this, you can "dirty" the seam with correction fluid (see the sidebar on the previous page).

If the solder doesn't flow properly, you can pickle the piece, re-flux, add new solder, and start again. This process can be repeated again and again until it works.

Now that you know the guidelines to successful soldering, let's begin.

Lightly flux the pieces to be soldered. Position the piece on a soldering high heat block exactly where you want it. Use a tiny brush or tweezers to put solder chips onto the seam where the two pieces will be joined, spacing them approximately ⅛ inch (3 mm) apart. It might be tempting to use more, but too much solder can get messy, resulting in hours of cleanup.

First, heat the area around the piece to gradually dry out the moisture in the flux. Once it's dry you can start to heat the actual metal. The flux will move through different color stages: from white to gray, then to glassy clear. When it goes clear, put the flame directly on the seam and solder area, heating both pieces evenly. Solder will follow the heat, so if one piece is hotter than the other, the solder will flow all over versus making a nice seam. You can heat the opposite side of where the solder chips are placed, thus drawing the solder through to the heated side. When the solder flows down the seam, it looks like a molten silver line. Remove the flame as soon as you're pleased with the join. Be cautious and don't overheat the metal, as too much heat can create fire scale—a purplish-gray stain on your sterling metal. Quench the piece in water, and then place it into a warm pickle pot.

Pickle will remove the oxidation. Mix the solution according to the manufacturer's instructions. Pickle works much faster when it's warm, so many folks keep it in a crock pot. Be sure to mark the outside of the pot to indicate it shouldn't be used for food. Once the pickle has removed the oxidation, use copper or bamboo tongs to pluck your piece from the solution. Rinse it in water, and then scrub it with pumice and a toothbrush. It's now ready for either another soldering operation or patina.

Placing solder chips

Flux the pieces

The flux begins bubbling

The flux is glassy clear, and the solder chip balls u

Fusing

You can only **fuse** with fine silver. That's because it's pure silver and the metal bonds easily when it melts. For an interesting effect, you can fuse scraps of fine silver to fine silver sheet. Many of the projects in this book use fused rings. Depending on the gauge of wire, you can use the rings as they are (as seen in the Tassel Necklace on page 52) or make them into a chain.

Rings

So let's fuse some rings. Start by making a jump ring (page 31) and check to make sure the ends fit together perfectly. Lay the rings on your heat resistant block so they're all uniform: with all the cut openings facing up and with enough space between them so that you won't accidentally melt the ring. I've found fusing rings to be a little like playing skeeball, because you can get into a rhythm and work down the line of rings, repeating the motion with the torch. This is what works for me, and as you get to know the process, I'm positive you'll discover your own tricks.

Set your torch so the flame's not fluffy, but not super intense and sharp either. Holding the torch above a ring, quickly trace over the ring with the torch to heat it evenly. It's important to keep the flame moving so you don't prematurely melt the silver. When the ring starts to turn pink, move the flame to where the ends of the ring meet and make short arches back and forth over the opening. The metal should turn molten and fuse together very rapidly. Remove the flame immediately when you see the ends fuse together. Quench the rings in cool water. If I'm fusing a lot of rings (like for making a chain), I take breaks in between so I can stay focused. It's usually when I let my mind wander that I melt a ring. If you notice the heat is bothering your eyes, you can wear safety glasses.

Fusing fine silver rings

CUES FROM CANDIE

If need be, extra solder can be removed with a needle file or sandpaper. To speed up the cleaning process, try using a flexible shaft fitted with an abrasive wheel.

The solder is flowing down the seam

Remove the torch and quench the piece in water

Balled-up wires

Balled-up wires make great head pins that you can leave as is or texture with a hammer. Copper, sterling, and fine silver wires can all be balled up on the end. Use a third hand to hold the wire on your soldering pad. Position the hottest part of the torch's flame at the end of the wire and gently heat, just above the end of the wire—the wire should zip up into the beginnings of a ball shape. Slowly move your flame around in a tight circle and move upward. The tiny ball will follow the heat upward and grow in size. If you're balling up larger-gauge wires, like 16 gauge, you may need to place a piece of heat safe block behind the wire to keep the heat contained.

Balling up a wire

The ball is fully formed

FORMING AN EAR WIRE

Making your own ear wires is easy, inexpensive, and, best of all, adds so much personality to your earring creations. You can make them simple with clean lines or decorative with spirals and beads—or anything in between.

Use half-hard 20-gauge wire to make strong ear wires. For a simple French ear wire with a balled end, cut $2^1/2$ inches (6.4 cm) of wire. You can opt to hammer the ball for a decorative element. Make a loop at the balled end of the wire; this is where your beaded elements will hang. Place the loop on the side of your mandrel, and roll the remaining wire around it. Make a gentle bend on the back half of the wire, and finish the end by twirling a cup burr over it. Lay the ear wire on your bench block, and hammer the top round section (that sits in your ear) with the flat side of a chasing hammer, thus work-hardening the metal. Now you can apply a patina or polish with the polishing cloth.

MAKING A LOOP-IN-LOOP CHAIN

Use your round-nose pliers to stretch a fused ring into an oval, keeping each one consistent with the previous one. Try to position the ring so the seam that you fused closed is in the middle; this way if there are any sorts of imperfections (lumps), they'll be less noticeable. If a link snaps open, you can re-fuse it (no pun intended). Next, pinch the middle of the oval closed so the ring forms a figure eight. Hold the center of the oval with round-nose pliers, and push the sides up until they're even with each other. At this point if you want your links to be wider, you can slide an awl or scribe in either side of the loop to open it up. Repeat to make another link. Slide one end of the loop into the last to start the beginning of the chain. Repeat to add additional links.

For a hammered variation, after you've opened up the loops on your links with an awl, lay a loop part on your bench block and hammer it with the flat side of your chasing hammer. Repeat for the opposite side. The hammering can harden the links, so you may need to anneal them before assembling the chain.

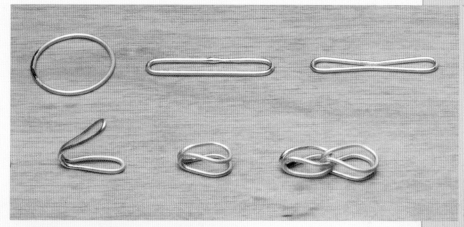

It only takes a few simple steps to make a link

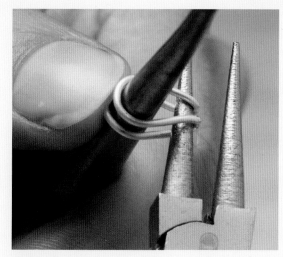

Widening a link

Applying a hammered texture

Finishes

As mentioned earlier, you can intentionally oxidize your metal pieces with **liver of sulphur**—a magical, but smelly solution. It comes in liquid or rock form. Use liver of sulphur on silver for a very durable patina that can range in color from gold all the way to black. Copper turns more brownish, then to black, and brass goes brown. Essentially, the longer you leave the metal in the solution, the darker the finish.

The process is easy. First make sure the metal is free of dirt and oil; otherwise the liver of sulphur won't take to the surface. Then working in a properly ventilated area, mix the solution according to the manufacturer's instructions. You can choose to either simply drop your metal piece in the container, or hold it with tweezers and dip it until the desired color is achieved. A fresh batch of liver of sulphur will work much faster than one that's been sitting for a day. It's a good idea to have a bowl of cold water sitting next to the solution so you can rinse your piece off quickly once you're happy with the effect. Give the piece a final rinse in cold soapy water. Completely oxidized surfaces will turn chalky and eventually flake off. To prevent this from happening, brush with a brass brush and a few drops of dishwashing soap. Use pumice powder and a touch of water to remove the oxidation from the high spots. If kept in a light-safe container (found in photo supply stores), the liver of sulphur solution can be used for a few days.

Use your **torch on copper** to achieve an iridescent patina. Just adjust your flame so it's light and fluffy, and gently dust it over the metal's surface. Stop when you like the look.

A haphazard red color can be applied to copper with a torch and a **pot of boiling water**. Position the pot of boiling water next to your torch. Hold your piece with tweezers, and then use the torch to heat the copper to a very hot red color. Keep the piece that color while you move it over the pot of boiling water. Get as close to the water as you can while still maintaining the red color, then drop the piece into the

You can achieve a wide range of color finishes using liver of sulphur

water. The water will bubble and pop quickly; you'll know the piece is ready to take out when it stops. Don't like the look? Throw it in the pickle, and try again once the piece is clean.

Copper plating is interesting to experiment with because you can create different layers and effects on your brass or silver surfaces.

To copper plate, make sure the metal to be plated is clean. You'll also need some pickle that has been well used—the color should be bluish because there are copper ions in it. If you don't have used pickle handy, drop some copper pieces into the new pickle. Wrap thin steel wire a few times around your metal piece. Are you having an eighth grade science class flashback yet? Place the piece in the pickle and wait until it's coated with a layer of copper. Your pickle is still perfectly usable when you pull the steel wire from it.

The following are a few ideas to try: copper plate brass or silver, then scratch away the copper finish using coarse sandpaper. This will reveal the brass or silver-colored metal underneath. Another option is to color the finish with liver of sulphur.

Metal paints are a fast and dazzling way to add color to your metal pieces. Check out the hobby shop for mini cans of spray paint used for model painting. There are also brush-on metal paints. Earrings, brooches, and pendants are all good candidates for painting because they tend to be worn in low traffic zones on our bodies, whereas rings and bracelets are susceptible to bumps and scrapes.

Polishing

There are a few ways to brighten up your metal once the fabrication is done. Polishing can range from pretty easy to labor intensive. The projects in this book were shined up with a simple inexpensive brass brush from the jewelry supply store. It's tempting to grab a **brass brush** from your local hardware store, but the bristles on those hurt when they run across the tops of your fingers! Brass brushing is your last step after pumicing and cleaning. Apply a drop of dish soap to the brush bristles and brush over your piece. Instead of scrubbing back and forth, your brush's life will be longer if you go in an upward direction each time (as you would with a file).

A hands-free way to polish is with a **tumbler**. And yes, when I first started, I used my faithful rock tumbler from my childhood. I'm a fan of stainless steel shot, a drop of dish soap, and about a ¼ cup (60 mL) of water in the tumbler. Just put your metal pieces in the tumbler for 30 minutes or more, and walk away. The pieces come out bright and shiny; just give them a rinse and pat dry.

Lastly, a yellow **polishing cloth** works wonders over a metal piece. I once heard a jewelry maker say, "the harder you work, the better it looks" while polishing. It's so true when using a polishing cloth. Rub one generously on a piece to achieve a high shine.

bamboo bail

Donut pendants come in so many interesting materials that I wanted to create a bail that you could see through in parts to the donut beneath. Also the bamboo design goes with the coloration of the stone.

WHAT YOU NEED

- Toolbox (page 12)
- Pattern (page 126)
- 20-gauge silver sheet metal, 3 x 1 inch (7.6 x 2.5 cm)
- ⅜-inch (9.5 mm) dowel rod
- Shish-kebab skewer
- Masking tape
- 2-inch (5 cm) donut bead
- 18-gauge copper-colored wire
- 49-strand nylon-coated beading wire, .018 diameter
- Random assortment of beads
- 18-gauge fine silver wire
- Riveting hammer
- Seed beads
- Scrimp closure findings
- Double drilled gold coral bead, 25 mm x 6 mm

HOW TO MAKE IT

Make the bail

Transfer the bail template to the silver sheet metal, and saw out the outside and inside shapes. Go easy sawing around the base of the leaves because those areas need to stay attached to the base piece.

File and sand the bail inside and out to a 600 finish. Find the center of the bail, and lay it over the top of the dowel rod. Fold the two sides down so they meet. You may have to lay the piece on a steel bench block and gently tap the sides to align it. If it's being stubborn, you can always anneal it and make some more forming tweaks.

Push the leaves outward with the skewer or something similar. Once they're raised slightly, you can pull them from the front. Careful; there may be sharp edges on the tips of the leaves. Protect the surface around the leaves with masking tape and then sand the tips.

Put the piece in liver of sulphur, and pumice the surface of the bail. Leave the inside oxidized and a darkened area on the leaves. Use a brass brush, or tumble the piece to shine it up.

Slip the donut bead between the two ends of the bail, and secure the bail ends together using three 8 mm jump rings made from copper-colored wire. Scuff the jump rings with sandpaper to make them look worn.

bamboo bail

Beading

Select some beads that complement the donut bead, and string them in your desired order and length. This piece has a whimsical random order combining chunky beads with delicate seed beads and pearls. Mixing shiny and natural surfaces alongside focal beads adds contrast and interest.

Clasp

Make a ⅝-inch-diameter (1.6 cm) ring with fine silver wire, and fuse the ends together. Hammer half the ring with the flat face of a chasing hammer. Texture the whole ring with a riveting hammer. Patina with liver of sulphur, and pumice away the raised areas of the ring. Finish by brass brushing. If you'd rather, oxidize the silver-plated scrimp findings and brass brush.

String one scrimp finding onto the beading wire followed by 11 seed beads. String the ring onto the wire, and thread the tail back down through the scrimp finding so the seed bead loop holds the ring in place. Remove the slack and tighten the screw in the scrimp finding.

Repeat for the toggle side to connect the gold coral bead.

From My Sketchpad

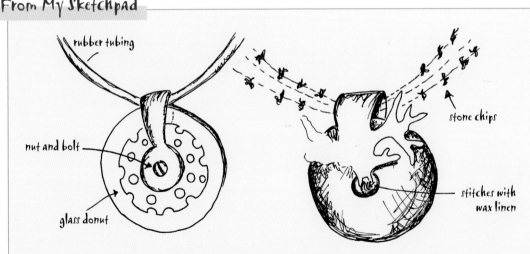

rubber tubing

nut and bolt

glass donut

stone chips

stitches with wax linen

woven copper necklace

Copper and turquoise are the perfect complement to each other. I like how the varied and irregular shapes of the beads work with the thin, undulating copper wire.

woven copper necklace

WHAT YOU NEED

- Toolbox (page 12)
- Pattern (page 125)
- 18-gauge copper
- Permanent marker
- #67 drill bit
- Copper tubing, $\frac{5}{32}$ diameter
- Shallow cavity doming block and punch
- #65 drill bit
- Riveting hammer (optional)
- 24-gauge copper wire
- Assortment of turquoise beads, 3 to 6 mm
- 18-gauge copper wire
- Two 18-gauge copper jump rings, $\frac{5}{16}$ inch (8 mm)
- 18-gauge copper jump ring, $\frac{5}{16}$ inch (8 mm)
- 19-strand beading wire
- Crimp beads
- Crimp covers (optional)
- Copper spacer beads, 6 mm
- Round copper beads, 3 mm

HOW TO MAKE IT

Make the square

Transfer the square template to the copper, and saw it out. Mark hole placements around the square with a permanent marker—the spacing between each hole is approximately 2 mm. Do not position any holes directly on the corners. Drill the holes using a #67 bit. Drill holes in the top right and left corners. If you want to add tube rivets, remember to start with a small drill bit size and work up to the $\frac{5}{32}$ bit.

Put the square in a shallow cavity in the doming block, and dome.

Create the spacer bars

Saw six $\frac{11}{16}$ x $\frac{3}{16}$-inch (1.7 cm x 5 mm) strips of copper. Use a #65 bit to drill three holes, spaced evenly apart, in each spacer bar. File and sand all the pieces, taking extra care to remove any sharp corners from the spacers. If you'd like, hammer the edges of the spacer bars with a riveting hammer to add some texture.

Weaving

Cut several 20-inch (50.8 cm) lengths of 24-gauge wire. It's key to anneal the wire before you weave it into the square; otherwise, it will work harden as you are weaving and snap.

You'll begin with weaving all the horizontal wires. As if you were making a knot at the end of thread, make a small loop at the end of the 24-gauge wire. With the loop side at the back of the square, thread the wire through a hole on the back corner and bring it through to the front.

Add a few beads to the wire, and thread it through the hole that's directly opposite of where the wire comes up.

Bring the wire back to the front at the next adjacent hole. String on another one to three beads, and put the wire back through the hole that's directly across the square on the other side. Continue this process until you reach the end. If you run out of wire, make a small loop or bend at the end to secure it in place and start a new piece.

Now for the tricky part—weaving through all the vertical wires. Secure a wire on the back as you did before and bring it through to the front. Weave the wire in an "over, under, over, under" fashion through all of the horizontal wires. During this step you can add more beads to the wire, if you like. The spots where the wires intersect lock the beads in place.

Once the piece is finished you can dip it quickly in the liver of sulphur to dull the copper color a bit.

The other findings

To make the clasp, create a hook and a 10 mm ring out of the 18-gauge wire. These two pieces and the 18-gauge jump rings can be hammered to add texture. Connect the 5 mm jump ring to the loop on the hook finding.

All of these findings can be oxidized in the liver of sulphur. Pumice and brass brush.

All together

Connect the jump rings to the two holes on the square. Cut six pieces of beading wire, each 9 inches (22.9 cm) long. Secure the beading wires to the jump rings with crimp beads. Optionally, you can cover the crimp beads with the crimp covers.

String 1 inch (2.5 cm) of turquoise beads onto one of the wires, followed by the appropriate hole on the spacer bar. String spacer and round copper beads onto the other two wires until they are equal to the first and the bar lies nicely.

String 2 inches (5 cm) of beads followed by the spacer bar onto the wires. Repeat with another 2 inches (5 cm) and a spacer bar.

String ¾ inch (1.9 cm) of beads onto the wires, and secure the end of the wires to the clasp findings with crimp beads—finishing with crimp covers, if desired.

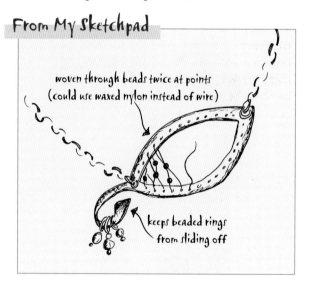

From My Sketchpad

woven through beads twice at points
(could use waxed nylon instead of wire)

keeps beaded rings
from sliding off

pomegranate earrings

The serpentine ear wire mimics a vine—perfect for hanging any fruity shape. I applied a patina to the commercial silver beads to add to the handmade look.

WHAT YOU NEED

Toolbox (page 12)

20-gauge half-hard sterling wire, 8 inches (20.3 cm)

$^{11}/_{16}$-inch (1.7 cm) dowel rod

Vise

6 black glass pearls, 4 mm

Cup burr (optional)

Adhesive (optional)

20-gauge dead soft sterling wire

Third hand tool

2 transparent pink glass beads, 10 mm

2 silver leaf bead caps

2 cubic zirconia droplet beads, 6 mm

2 silver jump rings, 5 mm

HOW TO MAKE IT

Note

I like to work each step on each ear wire at the same time to keep the pair looking the same.

Ear wires

Cut the 20-gauge wire in half so you have two 4-inch (10.2 cm) pieces. Make a simple loop at one end of the wire with round-nose pliers. Place the $^{11}/_{16}$-inch (1.7 cm) dowel rod in a vise, and position the loop in the center underneath the rod. Use the dowel rod to curve the wire (like a snake) back and forth twice. Add glass pearls, referring to the illustration for placement.

Bend the remaining wire with your thumbs to make a nice curve at the back of the wire. Trim the excess length from the end of the wire, and remove any sharp edges with sandpaper or a cup burr. If the glass pearls are sliding around, a touch of adhesive on the ear wire will hold them in place.

Fruit dangles

Cut two 1¼-inch (3.2 cm) pieces of 20-gauge dead soft wire. Place a wire in the third hand tweezers, and ball up with the torch. Clean the wires in the pickle. Thread a pink bead and a bead cap onto the wire, and finish with a wrapped loop.

Connect the droplet bead to the wrapped loop with a jump ring. Place all the components in the liver of sulphur to oxidize. Pumice the leafy bead caps and brass brush all the parts, leaving them a gunmetal color. Open the loop on the ear wire, and connect the beaded dangle.

Toggles are my favorite kind of clasp to use when stringing beads. This themed bee and flower toggle is made with brass and sterling to set the flower apart from the bee.

bee & blossom toggle

Toolbox (page 12)

Patterns (page 126)

18-gauge brass sheet

18-gauge sterling sheet metal

#55 drill bit

Shallow cavity doming block and
    punch set

Easy and extra easy solder

Torch

Flux

Third hand tool

18-gauge sterling jump ring, 5 mm

49-strand beading wire, .018 diameter

Beads

36 round tourmaline beads, 4 mm

32 brass floral bead caps, 5 mm

16 green freshwater pearls, 6 mm

8 copper-colored side drilled glass
    leaves, 10 x 5 mm

4 crimp beads

Copper crimp bead covers (optional)

Tip

When soldering the ring, think about which way you want the toggle to lay, and solder the ring so it's not at a pivot point.

HOW TO MAKE IT

Make the toggle

Transfer the flower and bee patterns to the appropriate sheet metals, and saw out. Center punch and drill the holes in the flower, and pierce out. Saw the body and wing pieces for the bee. File and sand the parts to 600-grit finish.

Texture the bee's wing area with a center punch.

Dome the flower shape in the dapping block. If desired, you can texture the flower by taking small circular motions with 150-grit sandpaper over the surface.

Solder the bee's wings to the body with easy solder. Use the third hand to hold the jump ring to the back of the bee body—slightly offset the ring. Flux and solder with extra easy solder.

solder chip

Patina both of the pieces with liver of sulphur, and pumice away just the wings so that the center-punched dots pop out. Finish with brass brushing.

Stringing

Connect two pieces of beading wire to the petals on the flower. String onto each of the wires: three tourmaline beads, bead cap, pearl, bead cap, leaf, bead cap, pearl, and bead cap. Repeat three more times, and finish with six more tourmaline beads. Connect the wires to the bee with crimp beads. Cover the crimp beads with copper crimp covers, if desired.

From My Sketchpad

jump ring

beads

solder ring so it's not
on a pivot point in loop

fiesta flower

Brightly colored, twirling skirts seen at a fiesta were the inspiration for this brooch. Whether you choose beads on a string or strips of fabric, you can weave just about anything in between the spokes of this piece.

Toolbox (page 12)

Pattern (125)

18-gauge silver sheet, 2¾ inches square (7 cm)

Shallow cavity doming block and punch

Sterling tie tack finding

Easy solder

Flux

Torch

22-gauge silver wire

Assortment of beads, including seed beads up to 4 mm

Tip

Placement of beads and colors next to each other is similar to making a crocheted ripple blanket in that all the colors have to work together. Sometimes colors can clash or look muddy next to each other, so it's good to place a strand of the desired bead row around the previous row before committing them to the wire.

Create the flower form

Transfer the flower template to the metal. Center punch and then drill a hole inside each of the petals. I like to saw the inside petal shapes first and finish with the outside. File the inside and outside edges and sand to 600-grit finish.

Set the flower shape over a shallow cavity on the doming block and the punch in the center of the flower. Strike the punch with a mallet and repeat, repositioning the flower in between strikes.

Solder the tie tack to the back center section of the flower. Pickle the piece.

Weaving the beads

Cut a 15- to 18-inch (38.1 to 45.7 cm) piece of 22-gauge wire. Starting next to the center, wrap the wire around a spoke to anchor it, hiding the tail on the backside. String a few beads equal to the width of the petal. Bring the wire up over the next spoke, down, and up through the previous petal. Repeat for each petal until you have made a complete round.

Continue adding beads and working outward until you're satisfied with the design. Wrap the wire twice around a bar and hide the tail on the backside. If you'd like, you can oxidize the piece with liver of sulphur and then polish it with a brass brush. Take care to not chip or alter the beads while brass brushing.

tail goes through and around

next bead sits here

anchor

From My Sketchpad

Weaving fabric strips or fibers with beads stitched on later.

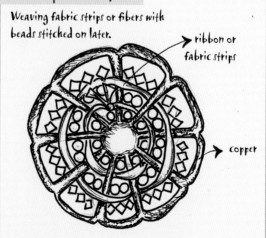

ribbon or fabric strips

copper

tassel
necklace

This dramatic piece can be worn either long or doubled up. I framed lava beads with fused and hammered rings as well as reticulated bead caps. Use as many kinds of chain as you like to create a unique tassel.

❀

WHAT YOU NEED

Toolbox (page 12)

18-gauge sterling silver sheet

Circle template and scribe or disc cutter tool

#55 drill bit

Dapping block and punch set

32 inches (81.3 cm) of 18-gauge fine silver wire

Torch

20 inches (50.8 cm) 18-gauge silver wire

30 assorted pieces of chain, each 2 to 2½ inches (5 to 6.4 cm) long

Lava rock pendant, 40 mm

Round lava rock beads, 16 mm

Ceramic black and white rondell beads, 8 mm

Round black beads, 6 mm

20-gauge silver wire

40 inches (1 meter) small cable chain, 2.3 mm

40 inches (1 meter) curb chain, 4.1 mm

Silver jump rings, 5 mm

HOW TO MAKE IT

Make the bead caps

Cut seventeen ½-inch-diameter (1.3 cm) circles, two ⅜-inch-diameter (9.5 mm) circles, and one ⅞-inch-diameter (2.2 cm) circle from silver. It's not imperative that they be perfectly round.

Follow the instructions in the basics, and reticulate each of the circles. Typically, you would reticulate a sheet of metal and then saw out the circles. For an irregular edge, do it after you saw out the circles. Center punch and drill each of the centers of the circles with a #55 drill bit.

Dome each of the ½-inch (1.3 cm) circles in the dapping block so they fit the curvature of the black beads. The ⅞-inch (2.2 cm) circle must be domed quite a bit to allow it to come down far enough to cover where the chain is connected to the tassel.

The ⅜-inch (9.5 mm) circles that fit on the top and bottom of the lava rock pendant are first domed and then set on their side on the steel block and tapped with a plastic mallet to narrow the shape into an oval.

The rings

Cut twelve 2½-inch-long (6.4 cm) pieces of 18-gauge fine silver wire, and make each of them into a ring. Fuse the ends together and hammer with the round side of the chasing hammer.

tassel necklace

Tassel

Cut a 5-inch (12.7 cm) length of 18-gauge silver wire. Make the start of a wrapped loop at the end of the wire; the loop needs to be fairly large since it'll be holding multiple pieces of chain. String a random assortment of chains onto the loop. Finish the end with a single wrap around the loop.

String the large bead cap, then the small bead cap, oval bead lava rock pendant, and the other oval bead cap. Make the start of another wrapped loop, connect a ring, and close the loop.

Apply a liver of sulphur patina to all of the components and then pumice away the high spots. To easily brass brush the chain, wrap it around a dowel rod.

All together

Make a simple loop at the end of the 18-gauge silver wire. String a bead cap, lava bead, and bead cap onto the wire. Repeat seven more times.

String a ceramic bead, black bead, and a ceramic bead—these should be nearly the same length as the silver rings. Make seven of these bead links.

Cut a 1½-inch (3.8 cm) length of 20-gauge wire, and ball up the end. String one black bead and ceramic bead, and finish with a loop. Connect this beaded dangle to the ring above the tassel pendant.

Start at the ring above the pendant and work both sides of the necklace. Connect a 1-inch (2.5 cm) piece of cable chain and a 1-inch (2.5 cm) piece of curb chain with a 5 mm jump ring. The beaded dangle should hang in between the two chain pieces.

bead link

Use a jump ring to connect the two chains to a ring and ceramic bead link. Open a loop on the lava rock bead and connect it to the ring and ceramic bead link. Repeat for the opposite side of the lava bead link.

Cut four 1¾-inch (4.4 cm) pieces from both the cable and curb chains, and connect them to the last ring with a jump ring. Open a loop on a lava rock bead link and connect it to the two chains. Repeat for the opposite side of the bead link and opposite side of the necklace.

Connect a ring to the end of the chains with a jump ring. Open a link on a lava bead link and connect the link to the chain. Open the opposite link and connect a ceramic bead link and ring. Connect another lava rock bead and ring.

Cut a 3-inch (7.6 cm) piece from both the cable and curb chains. Use a jump ring to connect them to a ceramic bead link ring. Repeat for the opposite side.

More Ideas

fun bead caps made from colorful tin

earring variation

old shanghai lantern earrings

In order not to take away from these awesome lampworked beads, I made simple domed bead caps and squared-off ear wires. Sometimes less really is more.

WHAT YOU NEED

- Toolbox (page 12)
- Scribe or permanent marker
- Metal cutting shears
- 22-gauge silver sheet, 2 x 2½ inch (5 x 6.4 cm)
- Metal cutting shears
- #65 drill bit
- Steel dapping block and punch set
- 20-gauge half-hard wire
- Torch
- 4 copper/brass spacer beads, 5 mm
- 2 lampwork beads, 12 mm diameter
- 2 sterling spacer beads
- 2 round brass beads, 2 mm
- Rubber tubing (optional)
- Cup burr (optional)
- Epoxy (optional)

Tip

Keeping the metal for the bead caps on the thinner side helps to keep the weight down, especially good when using heavy glass beads like these.

HOW TO MAKE IT

Bead caps

Use a scribe or permanent marker to trace four $^{11}/_{32}$-inch (9 mm) circles onto the 22-gauge silver sheet, then cut them out with the shears. Round and smooth the edges with a file. Find the center on each of the discs, and center punch. Drill each hole with a #65 drill bit, and sand the discs to 600-grit finish.

Place a disc into a fairly shallow cavity of the dapping block, and punch. Check the piece to the bead often until you get the desired fit.

Earrings

Cut two 3½-inch (8.9 cm) pieces of 20-gauge wire. Ball up each wire's end, and quench. Pickle and then set them aside.

Hammer the ball at the end of the wire with the round side of the chasing hammer.

Place the wires, metal beads, and bead caps in the liver of sulphur solution. Once oxidized, pumice the metal beads and wires but leave the bead caps totally oxidized. Finish by brass brushing all the pieces.

String a copper/brass spacer bead, bead cap, lampwork bead, bead cap, spacer, silver spacer, spacer, and brass bead onto a balled up wire. If the lampwork bead jiggles around, you can insert a piece of rubber tubing into the hole and cut it off flush with the bead to make the hole smaller.

old shanghai lantern earrings

Hold the wire 1¼ inches (3.2 cm) (or wherever you choose) above the hammered ball with chain-nose pliers, and make a bend. Move back ⁵⁄₁₆ inch (8 mm), and make another bend.

Use your thumbs to make a slight bend on the backside of the wire. Depending on how long you want to leave it, the end of the wire may need trimming. Remove rough spots and round out the end of the wire using sandpaper or a cup burr.

bend here with thumbs

Note

Be aware that the beads will slide up and down the wire. While this really doesn't matter while they're being worn (thanks to gravity), take care when storing them because the beads can make their way around the wires and fall off into the depths of your jewelry box. You can prevent that from happening by placing some epoxy on the wire and gluing the beads in place.

From My sketchpad

soldered to long wire

finish end of wire with spiral to hold beads on

profusion ring

Big rings are fun to wear. This one
was inspired by a tropical garden
party with lots of funky plants like
Bird of Paradise and where champagne
was served on sterling trays.

✳

profusion ring

Toolbox (page 12)

Pattern (page 126)

18-gauge sterling sheet

#65 drill bit

Shallow cavity dapping block and punch set

Ring mandrel

22-gauge sterling wire

Beading wire

Black Delica seed beads

Crimp bead

Bead assortment (including Czech glass beads)

20-gauge gold-filled wire

Make the ring

Test the fit of the paper pattern to your finger. Make any necessary adjustments by adding or subtracting length to/from the middle section.

Saw out the pattern for the ring, and then pierce out the middle design. Center punch and drill the holes at each of the points. File the edges and sand the piece to 600-grit finish.

Place the end of the ring in a shallow cavity on the dapping block and slightly dome just the end. Repeat for the opposite side.

Place the center of the piece on the ring mandrel at the desired ring size. Wrap the two sides around the mandrel so the three corners are next to each other.

If desired, texture the ring with 150-grit sandpaper, and apply a liver of sulphur patina. Pumice away the high spots.

Lace it together

Essentially, you're going to make a laced section similar to that on a sneaker. See the diagram for the lacing path, and add seed beads in between. Secure the two ends with a crimp bead.

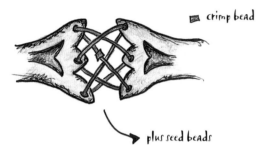

crimp bead

plus seed beads

Add the beads

To make the head pins, cut approximately twenty 22-gauge wires that measure 1 to 1¼ inches (2.5 to 3.2 cm) long, and ball up the ends with a torch. Finish by oxidizing with liver of sulphur.

If you've ever made a cha-cha bracelet or ring, this next part will be a cinch. If not, well then you must be persistent, and don't judge how it looks after attaching only a few dangles (like I almost always do). Start by choosing one focal bead, stringing it on a head pin, and finishing the end with a loop. Connect it to the center of the ring where the wires intersect—including both of the intersecting wires in the loop.

Continue stringing beads and attaching them to the wires around the focal bead. You can also form spirals out of the gold wire and attach them with head pins. These measure about ¼ inch (6 mm) in diameter. I hammered mine with the flat side of the chasing hammer on the bench block. With the botanical nature of this ring I felt like I was arranging flowers in a vase—you can tuck anything in from spirals to rows of seed beads!

From My Sketchpad

beaded dangles linked to chain

Vintage Bakelite bead held in place with tube rivets

domed earrings
& ring

I wanted to make a sharp-looking piece where the beaded elements could be changed easily to match moods and outfits. With this set you can complement everything from business attire to a T-shirt and jeans ensemble.

WHAT YOU NEED

Toolbox (page 12)
Pattern (page 126)
Scribe
18-gauge sterling silver sheet
Dapping block and punch set
#65 drill bit
2 silver jump rings, 4 mm
20-gauge half-hard silver wire
Easy solder
Torch
Cup burr
Bezel mandrel
18-gauge fine silver wire
2 black freshwater pearls, 6 mm
2 silver head pins, 1 inch (2.5 cm)
Sterling ring band, 5 mm width
Steel ring mandrel
Third hand tool
Clear or black beading elastic
Bead assortment

HOW TO MAKE IT

EARRINGS
The domes

Using the circle template, scribe two $^{17}/_{32}$-inch (1.35 cm) circles onto the silver. Repeat, scribing two $^{11}/_{32}$-inch (9 mm) circles. Saw out each shape, and square up the discs by filing. Sand the discs to 600-grit finish.

Dome each of the discs in the dapping block. Mark the center of each domed piece and drill with a #65 drill bit. Drilling from the inside out makes it easier to clean up the burrs on the back. Take it easy when drilling because the pieces may want to spin and get hot, making them hard to hold on to them. Do a little at a time and rotate out the discs, giving them time to cool in between.

The jump ring and pearl dangle hang from the large domed piece. Mark your hole placement so it's at least $^{1}/_{16}$ inch (1.6 mm) in from the edge. Center punch and drill with the #65 drill bit.

Clean up the burrs from drilling using sandpaper.

Cut two 2½-inch (6.4 cm) pieces of half-hard wire. Ball up the ends of the wire. Thread a wire through the small and then the large domed piece. Making sure there are no gaps, bend the wire 90° or so, following the curve of the outer dome.

domed earrings & ring

Flux the areas to be joined, and place solder chips along the wire. As you heat the piece, focus the flame more on the domed pieces because it'll take longer to bring those up to temperature. When I first started metalsmithing, I would get excited and heat the wires too early and end up with molten silver. Pickle and clean the pieces when you're finished soldering.

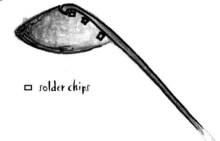

☐ solder chips

Position the earring piece up next to the bezel mandrel, and wrap the wire around to make a hook. Trim the wire to the desired length. Grasp the wire approximately ¼ inch (6 mm) from the end and make a slight bend outward. Sand or use a cup burr on the end of the wire so it's not sharp.

Dangles

Make two ¼-inch (6 mm) rings with 18-gauge fine silver wire and fuse the ends together. Round out the rings on a bezel mandrel and hammer them flat on the bench block.

Put all the findings and earrings in a liver of sulphur solution to oxidize them. Pumice the high spots and the ear wires. Brass brush or tumble.

Make balled head pins, string the pearls on, and finish with a loop. Connect a dangle to each of the fused rings.

Connect the fused rings to the domed earring pieces with 4 mm jump rings.

RING

Follow the instructions for making the two domed and drilled pieces and the balled wire in the earring instructions. The balled wire piece only needs to be approximately ⅝ inch (1.6 cm) in length.

Place the ring band on the steel ring mandrel and center punch the center of the band. Drill the hole with a #65 drill bit. Flux the areas to be joined, and drop the wire down through the two domed pieces and the ring. Use the third hand to hold on to the wire hanging down through the ring.

Place chips of solder on top of the ring band, around the base of the domed disc. When soldering, use the torch heat to pull the solder down through the hole where the wire goes. Pickle and check the soldered connection. You can repeat the process, fluxing and soldering where needed.

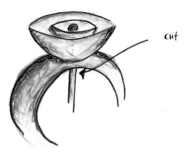

Cut the excess wire away inside the ring, and sand so it's flush. Oxidize the ring in liver of sulphur, and pumice away the edges on the domed pieces and band. Brush with a brass brush.

Bead rings

Make interchangeable decorative bead collars for the ring using elastic and any assortment of beads. Some of the beads shown here are freshwater pearls, coral cubes, and seed beads.

cut copper tubing necklace

Who would have thought tubing from a hardware store could result in this piece? Slices of copper tubing surround natural gemstones creating a classic look.

✿

WHAT YOU NEED

- Toolkit (page 12)
- ¾-inch (1.9 cm) brass tubing
- ½-inch (1.3 cm) brass tubing
- Riveting hammer (optional)
- Ring mandrel
- 20-gauge brass or gold-filled wire
- Brass chain
- Assortment of gemstones

HOW TO MAKE IT

Make the tubing rings

Using a small square of 320-grit sandpaper, sand the brass tubing (it's easier to do while it's a long tube versus after you've cut it). Repeat, moving down the grits to 600.

Mark your tubing into approximately ½ to ⅝-inch (1.3 to 1.6 cm) widths, and then saw into sections. Sand the edges of the tubing to remove any burs from sawing.

Slide each of the tubing pieces onto a ring mandrel, and texture with either a riveting or chasing hammer. While the piece is on the mandrel, you can center punch both sides—these holes are where you'll thread the wires when stringing.

When you drill the holes, a dowel rod that's slightly smaller than the tubing works well to support the rings. You can place it in a vise to free up your hands.

Sand the insides of the tubing pieces, removing burs.

cut copper tubing necklace

String it

The pieces are now ready for stringing. This particular
necklace uses simple loops to string each tubing piece
strung on a brass wire. The tubing beads make perfect
frames for anything from gemstones (like this necklace) to
found objects.

wire can be exposed

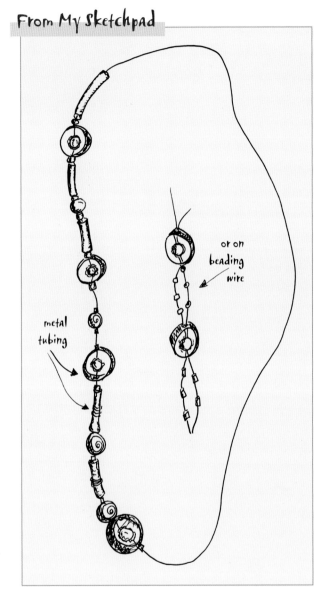

metal
tubing

or on
beading
wire

paisley interchangeable bracelet

I like versatility, and the lobster clasps on this piece allow for a quick strap change. Domed and riveted, the paisley focal piece is a great jumping-off point for a number of beaded bracelet combinations.

paisley interchangeable bracelet

WHAT YOU NEED

Toolbox (page 12)

Patterns (page 126)

18-gauge sterling sheet metal, 2¼ x 2-inch (5.7 x 5 cm) piece

20-gauge sterling sheet metal, 1 x 1½-inch (2.5 x 3.8 cm) piece

#65 drill bit

³⁄₃₂ drill bit (optional)

Dapping block and punch

20-gauge sterling wire, 3-inch (7.6 cm) piece

6 mm silver chain, 9-inch (22.9 cm) piece

3 sterling jump rings, 5 mm

3 lobster clasps, 12 mm

2 jump rings, 7 mm (one brass and one silver)

Sterling wire, 12-inch (30.5 cm) piece (for balled head pins)

Charm pieces

HOW TO MAKE IT

Make the paisley

Transfer the patterns; use the 18-gauge metal for the base piece and the 20-gauge for the smaller top piece. Saw the pieces out. File and clean up the pierced areas.

Drill the decorative holes on the scalloped edge with a #65 drill bit. Sand to a 600-grit finish.

If you like, you can make a beveled edge around each of the holes by twisting the ³⁄₃₂ drill bit back and forth in the hole while drilling—stop when you like the effect.

Create a stitch-like border around the small paisley piece by using a mini-screwdriver as a punch. Use a center punch to make dots under where the small paisley piece is connected.

WIRE WRAPPED TUBING BEADS

Almost any size tubing and wire can be used to make these funky little beads. The key is to anneal the spool of wire to be wrapped around the tubing. Cut your pieces of tubing to the desired thickness, and sand away any rough spots. Cut a 12- to 14-inch (30.5 to 35.6 cm) piece of wire, and thread one end through the piece of tubing, leaving just enough to have something to hold on to. Wrap the long end of the wire round and round the tube. If the wire gets too tough, you can anneal, pickle, and begin again. I used ¼-inch-diameter (6 mm) copper tubing and 22-gauge wire for these particular beads. A liver of sulphur patina and then some pumicing really brings out the linear texture.

Mark the holes where the rivets will go on the small paisley piece, and drill using a #65 drill bit.

Dome each of the pieces very slightly in a shallow cavity dapping block. Use the same cavity for each piece so they will all fit together perfectly.

Tape the small piece in the center of the big piece, and drill one hole through to the base piece. Drill the other holes, setting a rivet or a wire in place after you drill each hole so the pieces line up perfectly. Rivet each of the wires.

The charm bracelet

Cut one 3½-inch (8.9 cm) and two ⅝-inch (1.6 cm) sections of chain. Use a 5 mm jump ring to connect one end of the long piece to a lobster clasp. The two shorter pieces connect to the long section with two 7 mm jump rings—one brass and one silver. Connect lobster clasps to the ends of the two short sections using 5 mm jump rings.

Now it's time to go to town connecting your favorite whimsies for the charms. This piece has things like funky beads on balled-up wires, a hammered copper washer, an etched charm with a tubing rivet, and lots of hammered rings.

Charm ideas

More Ideas

Using a yard (.9 m) of 1 mm diameter leather, string a lobster clasp onto the middle of the cord. Even up the ends and make an overhand knot to lock the clasp in place. String chunky beads onto the leather, and separate them with knots. When you've reached the desired length, tie a lobster clasp to each end of the two tails. For added security, drop a touch of glue over the knots.

Swap out the band in a snap

dimpled earrings

Change things up a bit and try combining acrylic sheet with metal to create these modern earrings. The shiny silver against the matte black looks super.

❀

WHAT YOU NEED

Tool Box (page 12)

3/8-inch-thick (9.5 mm) black acrylic plastic, 1½ inch (3.8 cm) square

20-gauge sterling sheet metal, 1½ inch (3.8 cm) square

#65 drill bit

20-gauge sterling wire

Multi-purpose adhesive

Note

Cutting acrylic into shapes is a snap with your jeweler's saw; using beeswax is helpful. The smell of hot plastic can be strong and not so good for your health, so work in a well-ventilated area or wear a mask.

HOW TO MAKE IT

Scribe two 9/16-inch (1.4 cm) circles on the black plastic and saw them out. File the discs edges, shaping and removing the sharp corners.

Dip the pieces in water and sand with 600-grit paper to polish the surfaces and finish the edges. Find the center of each circle and drill with a #65 bit.

Cut two 7/16-inch (1.1 cm) sterling circles (don't worry if your circles aren't perfectly round) and sand them to a 600-grit finish. Find the center of the circle and drill with a #65 drill bit. Use a center punch (or other texturing tool) to texture the two pieces.

Ball up two ¾-inch (1.9 cm) 20-gauge wires. Thread the balled wire through the silver disc and the plastic piece, then rivet. Rest the balled up end on a hardwood block while you rivet so you don't flatten the balled head of the wire.

Drill a hole in the top edge of each of the discs. Make two ear wires and sand the ends where they will connect to the plastic pieces. Place a drop of multi-purpose adhesive into the drilled hole and insert the sanded end of the ear wire.

scuff with sandpaper and glue

gingko necklace

One day I was wondering if I could make fabric tubes to slide over rubber tubing, and this design began to emerge. The gingko leaf pendant came after I decided to use kimono fabric to cover the tubing.

WHAT YOU NEED

- Toolbox (page 12)
- Pattern (page 125)
- 18-gauge sterling sheet metal
- #51 drill bit
- #60 drill bit
- Wood dapping block and punch
- Bezel mandrel
- 36 inches (91.4 cm) of 22-gauge sterling wire
- 6 green glass droplet beads, 8 x 5 mm
- Kimono fabric (1 fat quarter)
- Sewing machine and thread
- Loop turning tool
- 10 inches (25.4 cm) of black rubber tubing, 6 mm diameter
- Fabric glue
- 7 lapis lazuli natural bead chips
- 135 red coral beads, 3 mm
- Crimp beads
- 49-strand, .018 diameter nylon-coated beading wire
- Silver French bullion wire
- 2 sterling cones, 15 x 6 mm
- 42 shell heishi beads, 5 mm
- 22 blue bicone crystals, 4 mm
- 20 yellow quartz beads, 6 mm

HOW TO MAKE IT

Gingko leaves

Transfer the large gingko leaf pattern to the sheet metal, and saw it out. The decorative holes were made by center punching and drilling with a #51 drill bit. File the nooks and edges to remove the teeth marks made from sawing. Sand the piece inside and out to a 600-grit finish.

Place the piece over a shallow cavity in the dapping block. Use the punch and mallet to dome the leaf section only, avoiding the stem.

Place the bezel mandrel in a vise, then wrap the stem section around the mandrel to create the bail. You may have to anneal the leaf if it becomes too difficult to bend. It also helps to use a plastic or rawhide mallet to tap the stem around the mandrel and to close the loop.

Clasp

Follow the same steps for the clasp, except this time drill the holes with a #60 drill bit. Curl the stem of the leaf under with round-nose pliers to make the hook part of the clasp.

Apply a liver of sulphur patina to all the leaf components, and pumice away the high spots. Brush with a brass brush or tumble.

Green bead dangles

String a green bead onto the 22-gauge wire so that 1 inch (2.5 cm) of wire sticks out from the side of the bead. Bend the wire straight up, and wrap the long end of the wire generously around the top section of the bead, and trim. Use your round-nose pliers to roll the 1 inch (2.5 cm) of wire down to make a loop.

roll down

wrap around

gingko necklace

Fabric tube
Cut a strip of fabric ¾ inch (1.9 cm) wide and 6 inches (15.2 cm) long. Fold the strip in half with right sides together and iron. Stitch down the length of the tube using a ⅛-inch (3 mm) seam allowance. Keep in mind that the actual seam will take up some space in the tube. Use a loop turner to turn the tube right side out. Slide the fabric tube over the rubber tubing. Secure the fabric on both ends with fabric glue.

Note
I'm no rock star on the sewing machine, but I want to warn you that because of its slippery threads and loose weave, kimono fabric is a bit difficult to make into a tiny tube. Any fabric will work, and there are many Asian-themed fabrics available on the market that would look equally as cool.

Gingko beaded dangles
Cut seven 1¼-inch-long (3.2 cm) pieces from the 22-gauge wire, and then ball them up. Apply a liver of sulphur patina to the wires, and lightly pumice. String one blue chip followed by a coral bead onto the wire. Use a wrapped loop to connect a dangle to each of the openings on the gingko leaf.

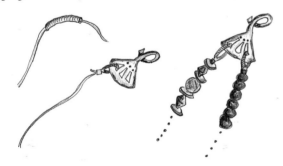

Coral strand
String one crimp bead and 49 red coral beads onto the beading wire followed by a green bead dangle. String six coral beads and another green bead dangle. Repeat four more times, ending with 49 more coral beads and

then a crimp bead. Cut four pieces of French bullion wire approximately 10 to 12 mm long. Dip them in liver of sulphur if you want a finish like the one on my piece. String one piece of French wire onto the beading wire and through the hole on the clasp. Run the end of the wire back through the crimp bead to remove the slack, and then crimp. Repeat for the opposite side.

Kimono strand
Dip the silver cones in liver of sulphur; pumice away the oxidation around the middle section and edges, and then brass brush.

String one heishi bead, a blue crystal, and a quartz bead onto the beading wire. Repeat this sequence nine times. String one more heishi bead and a blue crystal followed by a silver bead cone and the kimono fabric tube. Slide the large gingko pendant onto the tube. Continue stringing so the second half of the necklace mirrors the first. Connect the ends of the wire to the clasp as you did with the coral strand.

More Ideas

tubing bail

goldfish
in blue

Originally, I planned this to be the ulti-
mate goldfish…beaded with oranges and reds.
But after playing with color combinations, I
decided on a blue palette interspersed with
iridescent beads to evoke a watery feel.

❋

charmed tubing
necklace

Sterling tubing is adorned with tons of hammered jump rings and dangles. Use up random stones and metal beads to create the dangles. The contrast between knotted silk and copper chain against the charms is what makes this piece so captivating.

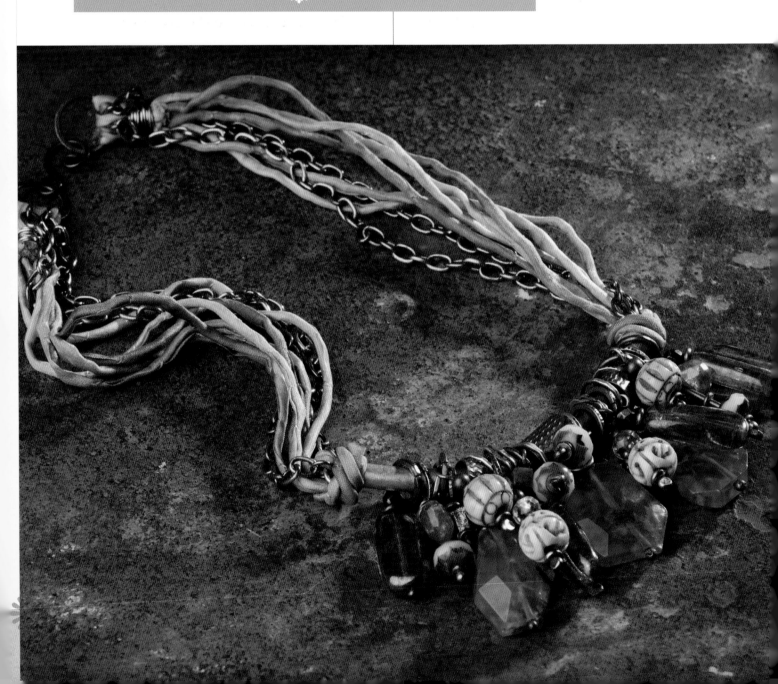

Toolbox (page 12)

20-gauge fine silver wire, 30 inches (76.2 cm)

20-gauge copper wire, 30 inches (76.2 cm)

20-gauge copper sheet, 1 x 1½ inches (2.5 x 3.8 cm)

Ferric chloride etching solution

Dividers

Pickle

Bezel mandrel

Flux

Medium and easy solder

Torch

Three 18-gauge copper jump rings, 6 mm

Heavy-wall sterling tubing, 5 mm OD/3.75 mm ID*

Tubing bender set

#65 drill bit

18-gauge sterling silver sheet metal (two small scraps that are just larger than the tubing end)

High heat block

Third hand tool

Two 18-gauge silver jump rings, 7 mm

5 mm link copper chain, four 5¾-inch (14.6 cm) pieces

Eight 18-gauge copper jump rings, 5 mm

3 silk strands, each 44 inches (111.8 cm) long

Two 16-gauge hammered copper jump rings, ½ inch (1.3 cm)

20-gauge half-hard sterling wire

Assortment of beads

20-gauge copper wire

* copper tubing would also work well for this piece

Note: Easily change the overall look of this piece with different silk cord, metal colors, and beads.

Rings

I formed the silver and copper jump rings from which the charms hang. They're slightly larger than the tubing. You can use any combination of metals that you'd like; I think an assortment keeps things interesting.

I also used wider, etched bails on the tubing. To make them, use a permanent marker or some other resist to transfer a design to the strip of 20-gauge copper. Follow the instructions in the Basics section to etch the copper.

Two of the copper strips measure ³⁄₁₆ x 1 inch (5 mm x 2.5 cm) and the other measures ½ x 1 inch (1.3 x 2.5 cm). Use your dividers to mark the lines on your copper, and then saw. File the edges so they square up. Anneal the copper strips, and then pickle. The ½-inch-wide (1.3 cm) strips are pretty easy to roll around the bezel mandrel to make a ring. You may have to tap the wider ring into place with a plastic mallet. Don't worry if your tubes make oval shapes. Once you solder them, they can be rounded out by putting them on a mandrel and tapping with a mallet.

Flux the inside and outside of the seam. Lay medium solder chips down the inside seam and carefully heat around the outside. When the solder flows, draw it through to the outside.

Solder an 18-gauge copper jump ring over the top of the center of the seam on each bail . This is so when a charm is hung from it, your solder seam won't show.

Tubing base

Make a slight arch in your tubing using the tubing bender. I pushed mine up against a round table leg to help form it. Saw the tubing so the arch is even and approximately 3 inches (7.6 cm) long.

Sand the ends of the tubing so they're flat. Carefully drill two holes on the backside of the tubing. It's a little challenging to drill tubing because of the round surface, but go easy and hold the bit really steady, and you can do it! The holes are to relieve the pressure when soldering the tube closed—believe me, you don't want the ends blowing off this thing.

charmed tubing necklace

Flux the two scraps of sterling sheet and the ends of the tubing. Place a sterling scrap on the high heat block. Use the third hand to hold the tubing down on the sterling. Place the medium solder chips around the seam, and solder. Pickle and repeat for the other side.

Carefully saw around the tube, removing the extra silver. The key is paying attention to all of the areas at one time and to not angle the saw, which could result in slicing through the tubing.

Wrap a strip of masking tape just under the edge of the sterling end piece, and file down the edge. The tape helps to protect the tubing from getting scuffed as you file.

Solder a silver 7 mm jump ring to the end of the tubing. Slide the rings and bails on in the desired order, and then solder the second jump ring on.

Finishing touches

Put the whole piece in liver of sulphur, and then pumice. I'm not going to lie to you: it took a LONG time to pumice away the raised areas and parts of the tubing, but it's worth it. Be sure to rinse the piece thoroughly.

Connect two pieces of copper chain to one end of the tubing and the opposite end to the large hammered copper rings with the 5 mm jump rings. Repeat for the opposite side.

Cut the three pieces of silk in half. Thread all three ends through one of the jump rings that is connected to the tubing, then even up the ends. Make an overhand knot with the silk so that the knot covers the jump ring on the tube.

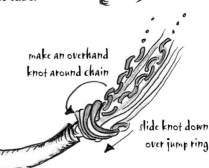

silk strands threaded through

copper chain connected

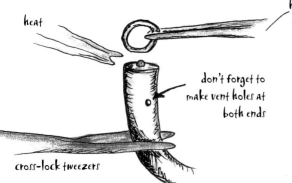

heat

hold jump ring with tweezers so it heats up and is ready to set in place when solder flows

don't forget to make vent holes at both ends

cross-lock tweezers

make an overhand knot around chain

slide knot down over jump ring

Repeat for the opposite side. Thread the ends of the silk through a large copper jump ring, and fold over. Even up the length with the copper chain, and wrap the two sides together with half-hard silver wire. If you want, you can patina the silver wire beforehand with liver of sulphur.

Create an assortment of beaded dangles strung onto balled-up copper and silver wires. There are no rules here—it can be symmetrical or asymmetrical. This piece has the heavier stones connected to the etched bails.

Clasp
Use the 20-gauge copper to make a wire hook.

From My Sketchpad

make the bail out of square tubing

dangly earring version

etruscan earrings

Simple metalworking techniques really set these beads off. The crosshatch scratching combined with an antiqued patina on the bead caps, hammered bead wires, and irregular rings give this pair an ancient feel.

WHAT YOU NEED

- Toolbox (page 12)
- 18-gauge fine silver wire
- Bezel mandrel
- Gold lampworked beads
- Circle templates
- 22-gauge sterling sheet
- Metal cutting shears
- #65 drill bit
- Steel doming block and punch set
- 20-gauge sterling wire
- 20-gauge half-hard sterling wire
- Cup burr (optional)

Tip

If the hole in a bead is too large, you can make it smaller with rubber tubing. Cut the piece of tubing so it's the same length as the bead's hole depth, apply some adhesive to the tubing, and insert into the bead.

cut tubing flush with bead

HOW TO MAKE IT

Make the rings

Cut two 1¼-inch-long (3.2 cm) pieces of 18-gauge wire. File each of the ends to remove the pinched edges. Bring the ends of the wire around to form a ring. Check to make sure there's a snug fit, and fuse the wire into a solid ring. Repeat for the other ring.

Stretch the ring over a mandrel to make it perfectly round. Now, this gets technical— make the ring an oval shape by gently "squishing" it between your thumb and index finger.

Hammer the rings with the flat side of a hammer on a steel block.

Bead caps

Get your lampworked beads handy, and slide a circle template over the bead to determine the diameter. Trace the circle size onto paper, and indicate the center with a dot. You can play around with different bead cap shapes and sizes. I opted for triangles here. Once you have your design on paper, cut it out and check it against the actual bead. All set? Duplicate the pattern three more times, and adhere them to the silver sheet. Use metal shears or a jeweler's saw to cut your shapes out of the 22-gauge sheet.

Center punch and drill the center of the bead caps with a #65 drill bit. File, sand, and finish the bead caps as usual, and then dome them just enough to match the curve of the bead. Apply a liver of sulphur patina. I added a scratchy crosshatch texture by lightly going over the cap surfaces in different directions with a coarse file.

etruscan earrings

Head pins
Ball up two silver wires. I hammered the balls on the wires quite a bit and then gently hammered the wire just enough to make it not so round. Don't worry if your wire doesn't quite fit the hole in the bead cap; the hole can be opened up a bit with a round needle-nose file.

Ear wires
Cut two 2½-inch (6.4 cm) pieces of half-hard wire. Ball up the wires and then pickle them. Flatten the balls at the ends of the wires with the flat side of the hammer. Make a small hook shape at the hammered end of the wire. Use a small bezel mandrel to form the ear wire, and then trim the end of the wire to your desired length. Sand or use a cup burr to round the end of the ear wire.

Patina
Put the wires and hammered rings in liver of sulphur, brass brush, and then texture with 220-grit sandpaper. Instead of texturing the ear wire, I used pumice to bring it back to a silver color.

Assembly
From the bottom up, string a bead cap, a bead, another bead cap on a balled-up head pin, and finish with a simple loop. Connect this loop to the hammered ring. Open the loop on the ear wire, and connect the ring. Repeat for the other earring.

midsummer's night

I can't think of a better way to show off a stunning art bead than by framing it with bead caps in a spring latch bracelet.

midsummer's night

Toolbox (page 12)

Polymer art bead, 22 x 6 mm

20-gauge sterling sheet metal

#55 drill bit

Heatless abrasive wheel for texturing

18-gauge fine silver wire

Spring latch bracelet finding

Doming block and punch set

18-gauge half-hard silver wire

20-gauge sterling wire

10 to 15 beads, assortment, 4 to 12 mm

20-gauge copper jump ring, 6 mm

HOW TO MAKE IT

Making the bead caps

Begin by creating a pattern for the flowery bead caps that will go on both ends of the polymer bead. The trick is to draw a circle on paper in the desired diameter of the bead cap. Then draw a smaller circle in the middle of the first, and mark the center. Draw approximately nine long, slender petals radiating out from the smaller circle. Slender petals are easier to wrap around the polymer bead, serving like prongs.

cut in fairly close to the center hole to make rolling the petals over easier

Saw out the flower shapes, and drill a hole in the middle of each with the #55 drill bit. File and sand around the edges of the petals. For a subtle texture, try the heatless wheel tool attachment for the flexible shaft. This can sometimes create rough spots, but those can be removed by lightly sanding with 600-grit paper.

Finish one end of the 18-gauge wire with a wrapped loop. String the wire through a flower bead cap, the polymer bead, and the other bead cap. The wire will help keep the pieces aligned while you roll the petals around the sides of the bead. If the petals are too hard to manipulate, you can anneal, pickle, and start again. When you are satisfied with the fit, finish the opposite end of the wire with another wrapped loop, taking care that the total length from end to end is smaller than the opening on the bracelet finding. This will give it tension to keep it latched while being worn. Put the piece in liver of sulphur, pumice, and brass brush.

width of beaded piece must be shorter than the bracelet opening

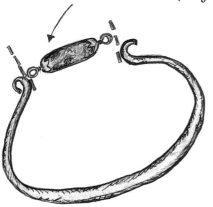

Texturing the bracelet finding

At this point, the commercial bracelet finding has a highly polished surface. But by now I bet you've figured out how much I love to alter surfaces with texture and patinas. I wanted the bracelet to match the bead caps, so I went over the surface with the heatless wheel, then gave it a light sand with the 600-grit sandpaper, and finished it off with the liver of sulphur patina. Massage the piece with a bit of water and pumice on your thumb to remove some of the patina. Finish by brass brushing.

Beaded dangles

Make a fused silver jump ring approximately 9 mm in diameter, and hammer it flat.

Cut five 1½-inch-long (3.8 cm) wires, and ball them up. String the beads in your desired order on the balled-up wires, and connect them to the silver jump ring with a wrapped loop.

Make another jump ring using copper wire measuring ¼ inch (6 mm), then hammer flat.

Put both of the rings in liver of sulphur. Lightly pumice and brass brush.

Open the ring on the bracelet finding and connect the polymer bead piece, copper ring, and silver beaded ring. Close the ring so it's secure.

From My Sketchpad

loaded- "cha-cha" effect

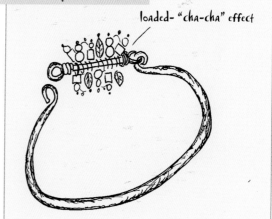

rustic chandelier earrings

Brass instead of copper, ovals in place of circles—by varying the shapes, metals, and finishing textures, these earrings easily take on an entirely new look.

WHAT YOU NEED

- Toolbox (page 12)
- 18-gauge fine silver wire
- 20-gauge fine silver wire
- 20-gauge copper wire
- Torch
- Ring mandrel
- Riveting hammer
- 20-gauge half-hard sterling silver wire
- 8 brass/copper spacer beads, 5 mm
- 4 copper round beads, 4 mm
- 4 lepidolite cube beads, 4 mm
- 2 quartz rondell beads, 6 mm
- Epoxy (optional)

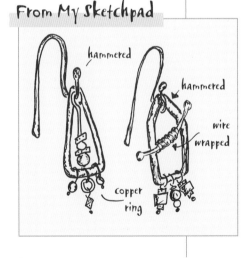

From My Sketchpad

hammered
hammered
wire wrapped
copper ring

HOW TO MAKE IT

Make the rings

Make two ¾-inch-diameter (1.9 cm) silver rings with the 18-gauge wire, and fuse the ends together. Repeat, making two rings, ⅜ inch (9.5 mm) in diameter with the 20-gauge silver wire. Make two copper rings, each measuring 9⁄16 inch (1.4 cm), and solder them closed.

Grasp the smaller silver ring with flat-nose pliers and squeeze. Repeat three more times to make a square-shaped ring. Repeat to make a second square ring.

Hammer the large ring with the riveting hammer, the copper ring with the flat face of the chasing hammer, and the square ring with the round side of the chasing hammer on the steel bench block.

Put it all together

Cut two 2-inch (5 cm) lengths of the 20-gauge half-hard wires. Make a loop at the end of the wire that's big enough to hold all the rings. String one copper spacer and round bead onto the wire, and finish the end in a French hook shape.

Cut six 1-inch (2.5 cm) 20-gauge wire pieces, and ball up the ends. If you'd like, hammer the balls with the rounded end of the chasing hammer to flatten them.

Put all of the components in the liver of sulphur solution, and let them oxidize. Pumice away the raised areas with a brass brush.

String one pink cube and spacer bead onto a balled-up wire, and finish with a loop. Repeat three more times. String one quartz bead followed by a spacer and a round copper bead onto a wire, and finish with a loop. Repeat.

Attach three beaded dangles to each of the large rings. Open the loop on the ear wire and hang the large ring, copper ring, and square ring.

If you notice the beads on the ear wire are moving up and down, add a drop of epoxy and slide the beads in place.

square bead cuff

This eye-catching piece is comprised of small coils and hammered square beads. The metal beads—like miniature mirrors—perfectly reflect the color of the crystals.

Toolbox (page 12)

20-gauge sterling sheet metal

Metal cutting shears

#65 drill bit

Dapping block

18-gauge fine silver wire

Copper tubing, ⅛- inch (3 mm) diameter

Mandrel

Balled-up head pins

Oval memory wire

Beads

Fuchsia square beads, 6 mm

Fuchsia round crystals, 4 mm

Quartz briolettes, 10 x 6 mm

Silver and black beads, 4 mm

Faceted lead colored glass beads, 4 mm

4 black/lead colored beads, 6 mm

Make the square beads

The silver metal squares measure 6 to 10 mm and are by no means square! Draw lines on the silver sheet, cut on the lines to make strips, and then cut the strips into squares (or close to).

Smooth the edges with a file.

Lightly sand both sides of the square, then hammer one side with the round side of the chasing hammer.

Center punch and then drill the middle of the squares with a #65 drill bit. Remove the burr on the back by sanding.

Since the metal is so thin, the squares can easily be domed in a dapping block without using much force.

Curly links

Make a loop at the end of the 18-gauge wire. With the loop pressed against the copper tubing, wrap it around two or three times— warning: this is a little hard on the thumbs. Finish the opposite side with another loop, and position them so they are parallel to each other. These are approximately ⁷⁄₁₆ inches (1.1 cm) long.

Spiral clasp

Form a nickel-sized spiral with the 18-gauge wire. Make a tight connection at the end, so that the wires lie side to side, and fuse them together.

Cut a 1¼-inch (3.2 cm) piece of silver wire, and ball it up. Roll the balled-up end around a small mandrel to make the hook, and finish the end with a simple loop. Position the hook and loop so they are perpendicular to each other.

square bead cuff

Put it together

Oxidize all of the silver pieces with liver of sulphur, and pumice away the high spots. Brass brush or tumble.

String one faceted lead-colored bead and one square pink shell bead on a head pin and finish with a wrapped loop. Do the same with a fuchsia crystal and silver square bead.

Create mini-pinch bails for the quartz briolettes with 20-gauge wire and chain-nose pliers.

Cut two pieces of the memory wire so they overlap approximately ¼ inch (6 mm). Make loops at the end of each wire.

Refer to the illustration below for assembly order.

Depending on your wrist size, you may have to adjust the length by taking away some of the beads. Finish the ends with loops.

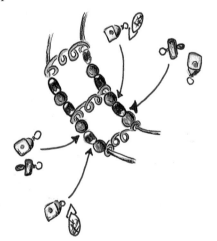

Connect the spiral part of the clasp to the loops on the end of the wires. Connect a curly link to the loops on the opposite wires. Open the loop on the hook part of the clasp, and connect it to the middle wrap on the curly link.

Tip

The beauty of this latch is its versatility; you can latch it in the center of the spiral or on the edge, which is great for sizing options.

cat's cradle

The surface
coloring of
this donut is
simple so an
intricate bail
works. Alter-
native beads,
such as small
crystals, gem-
stones, or
larger seed
beads, can be
used to change
the look.

✳

cat's cradle

WHAT YOU NEED

- Toolbox (page 12)
- 18-gauge fine silver wire
- 20-gauge copper wire
- Donut bead, 1½ inch (3.8 cm) diameter
- Bezel mandrel
- 24-gauge dead soft sterling silver wire
- Cream-colored seed beads, 11/0
- 18-gauge silver sheet
- 18-gauge silver jump ring, 5 mm
- Easy solder
- Torch
- Natural-colored leather cord, 1 mm diameter

Tip

If your donut bead is a different size, you can make a "test" loop out of copper wire to check the fit before using silver.

HOW TO MAKE IT

Make the bail

Cut a 5-inch (12.7 cm) piece of silver wire, form a circle, and fuse the ends together. Pinch the middle of the ring, bringing the sides together. Pull the two loops upward so they are even. Wrap an approximately ¼-inch-long (6 mm) piece of 20-gauge copper wire around the middle.

Thread the loop piece through the donut bead. Slide one side of the loop onto the bezel mandrel to slightly open it. Repeat for the opposite side.

Lay one side of a loop on the bench block and hammer with either side of the chasing hammer, depending on what texture you want. Repeat for the opposite side. Bend the two sides up so they are aligned.

Secure the bail to the donut by wrapping the top of the two loops together using 20-gauge copper.

Use the 24-gauge wire to wrap around the middle, just above the copper-wrapped area on the front side. Wrap the wire two to three times, and on the last wrap, string one seed bead. With the wire coming out from the back to the front, start weaving.

Weave the bail

The weaving path for the wire through the bail follows a figure eight. The seed bead placement is so that they "fit" together. After a few passes with the wire, you'll get a feel for when and how many seed beads to add.

Take the wire over and down through the opposite side of the bail and back to the front. Repeat, making a complete figure eight with the wire. String one seed bead on the wire, and take the wire down and around, back to the front. Make another figure eight without seed beads.

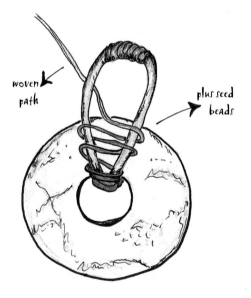

woven path

plus seed beads

From here to the end, each time the wire comes to the front, add a seed bead or two. Continue working the figure-eight pattern, and when you come to the end, anchor the wire as you did when you started.

Quick button clasp

Cut a ⅝-inch (1.6 cm) disc from the silver sheet. File, sand, and then texture the piece with a center punch, and dome it in the dapping block.

Flux the disc and the jump ring where the pieces will be joined. Solder the jump ring to the bottom center of the domed disc with easy solder. It helps to hold the jump ring with the third hand while you solder. Pickle the piece once you have a good connection, and then clean it with pumice.

Oxidize

Put the donut pendant and button clasp pieces into the liver of sulphur until they are black. Pumice away the high spots and brush with a brass brush.

Make a necklace

Cut two pieces of leather, each 32 inches (81.3 cm) long. Fold the pieces in half. Thread the looped end through the bail and then the two ends through the loop. Pull snug. Repeat for the opposite side. Make overhand knots down both sides of the leather (to your desired length). Fold the end of the leather to make a loop for the button to go through, and secure with an overhand knot. Wait to trim the ends until you finish the opposite side. Tie the button in place with a double knot. Add extra security to the clasp knots with a touch of adhesive.

geometric brooches

Several friends who knit told me how great these are for hand-knit scarves. They're simple to make, and you can select the beads to match your scarf.

WHAT YOU NEED

- Toolbox (page 12)
- Patterns (page 126)
- 18- to 20-gauge copper or sterling sheet metal
- Drill bits
- Permanent marker
- Hammers for texturing (chasing for silver, cross peen for copper)
- Wood doming block and punch
- Copper tubing, 5⁄32 inch (4 mm) (optional)
- Torch
- Pickle
- 18-gauge half-hard silver wire
- 20-gauge copper or sterling wire
- Bead, chain, and jump ring assortment

HOW TO MAKE IT

Transfer the pattern to sheet metal, then saw and file to remove the saw lines. Mark the hole placements with a permanent marker, then center punch and drill to your desired size. Sand the piece to 600-grit finish.

Texture the piece with your desired texture tool. The silver brooch has a planished texture, while the copper one was hammered with a forming hammer.

Place the piece in the wood doming block, and add a slight curvature using the punch and mallet. Now's the time to add decorative tube rivets and a patina of liver of sulphur, if you so desire.

Ball up the desired number of head pins and then pickle them. Clean and brass brush the head pins before stringing.

Embellish the brooches with jump rings, chain, and beads strung on the balled-up head pins. See the project photos for ideas.

From My sketchpad

pin stem is hammered

pierced holes with dangles — like "frames"

stitch-like to border texture

Make the pin stem

Cut a length of 18-gauge half-hard wire 3 to 5 inches (7.6 to 12.7 cm) long. Create a "stop" for the beads; a few twirls of your round-nose pliers will create a spiral, or use your torch to ball up the end of the wire. Both of these pin stems have been hammered and patinaed with liver of sulphur. String the beads on the wire and check the length of the pin stem. I like to leave about ¾ inch (1.9 cm) sticking out of the fabric at the end. If you leave it really long, I guarantee you'll harpoon yourself—speaking from experience here. File and sand a point on the end of the wire.

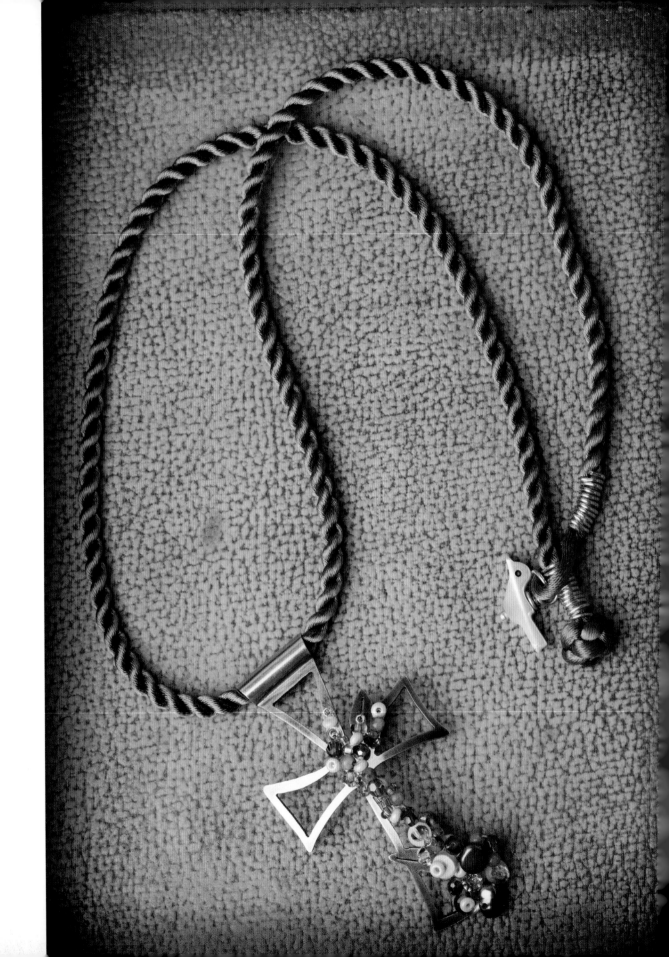

serene cross

"Morning Glory" beads twine up this simple pierced cross. I wrapped the ends of the cording with sterling wire and adorned the clasp with a peaceful dove.

WHAT YOU NEED

Toolbox (page 12)

Pattern (page 125)

18-gauge sterling silver sheet metal, 2½ x 1¾ inches (6.4 x 4.4 cm)

#67 drill bit

Shallow doming block and punch set

Heavy-wall sterling tubing, .197 "OD/ .147 " ID

Flux

Easy solder

Torch

Third hand tool

Pickle

12-inch (30.5 cm) piece of nylon cord, .35 mm diameter

Bead assortment: white seed beads, 3 mm blue crystals, blue freshwater pearls, blue cats' eyes

Rope cord

20-gauge dead soft sterling wire (optional)

HOW TO MAKE IT

Create the cross

Transfer the cross pattern to the silver sheet metal, and saw it out. Center punch and drill each of the holes with the #67 drill bit. File and sand to a 600-grit finish.

Dome the cross shape slightly in the doming block.

Cut the tubing for the bail so it's approximately ¼ inch (6 mm) longer than the top of the cross.

Flux the tubing and cross where they'll be joined with solder. Lay the tubing on your soldering block. Use the third hand to hold the cross on top of the tubing. Sometimes it's hard to make a tight join like this, so I push the third arm tool down and past where the cross will sit on top of the tubing. Then when you set the cross in place it creates some pressure, thus producing a tight join. Add your solder chips along the seam, and then solder. Pickle and clean.

Saw or file the tubing bail so it angles outward following the line of the cross. Oxidize the piece with liver of sulphur and pumice the surface, leaving the inside edges dark. Brass brush.

serene cross

Tie the 12-inch (30.5 cm) piece of nylon cord to the cross, and begin stitching the beads on in a free-form pattern. When you're finished, tie off the cord and secure the knots with a drop of adhesive.

cluster beads, stitching small seed beads and 3mm crystals around large beads

cord comes up and goes back down same hole

Slide the pendant onto a rope cord. Optionally, you can create a bead dangle to connect to the loop/clasp and wrap the ends with 20-gauge silver wire.

fanciful
feathered
friends

These whimsical guys—with their beaded tails—
are so fun to make. The sky's the limit when
it comes to what beads you can use.

❀

fanciful feathered friends

WHAT YOU NEED

Toolbox (page 12)

Patterns (page 125)

18-gauge sterling sheet in desired colors, 2½ x 3½ inches (6.4 x 8.9 cm)

³⁄₃₂-inch (2.5 mm) drill bit

⅛ inch (3 mm) fine silver seamless tubing, OD.058˝/ID.034˝, 3-inch (7.6 cm) length

20-gauge sterling half-hard wire, 22 inches (55.9 cm)

26-gauge sterling silver wire, 1-inch (2.5 cm) length

Medium, easy, and extra easy solders

Torch

Specific to each bird:

Brass Bird

¼ inch (6 mm) x 00-90 brass nuts and bolts and mini wrench tool set

#55 drill bit

Silver Bird

20-gauge sheet copper, 2 x 1½ inch (5 x 3.8 cm) piece

Hobby/model paint

#65 drill bit

HOW TO MAKE IT

For both birds

Transfer the body, wing, and beak patterns to the sheet metal, and saw the shape out. It's good if the beak is a little larger than the body pattern because you can file the sides so it fits perfectly after it's soldered. Use a ³⁄₃₂-inch (2.5 mm) bit to drill the holes for the eye and wing. A half-round file works great for cleaning up the curved edges around the bird shape. For the wing, drill the two holes in it first (see the materials list for specific bit size), then lay the wing on the bird piece and mark where the holes should go. Center punch and drill one hole. Position the wing, and thread a wire through both layers before you drill the second hole—this ensures that the holes match up perfectly on the two layers.

Making the pinback

Planning where and how your pin mechanism will go on the back of your piece is the most important part of this process. It must be placed above the centerline on the back of your piece, or else it'll tip forward when it's being worn.

Each project specifies how long the tubing and pin catch pieces should be. The "U" shape piece (the catch) is made with a thin strip of sheet metal, and a hinge is made from fine silver tubing. Sand a flat spot on the tubing so it doesn't roll around while you position it. Solder in place using extra easy solder. Position the hinge so the top of the tube aligns with the top of the catch. Solder using extra medium.

To make the pin stem, first file a groove into the top of your bench pin—the three-square needle file is good for this task. Taking into account where your pin stem needs to bend in order to lock into place at the hinge, figure out what length your 20-gauge half-hard wire needs to be. Cut the wire and lay it into the bench pin groove. Taper the end with a file, turning the wire as you go. Once a tip has formed, sand it, going through all the grits. Polish the end with a polishing cloth.

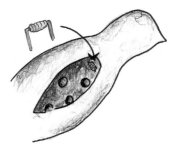

Position the wire so that the tip just barely peeks out the other side of the catch. Mark where the first 90° bend should be. Make the bend, slide the stem into the tubing, and make a second bend. Trim the wire, leaving a ½-inch (1.3 cm) length. If you want to get fancy, you can make a twirl at the end of the wire for a decorative touch. Place your index finger on top of the twirl and pull up on the long stem—this gives it spring. You can also push back on the stem just a little so that when it snaps into the catch it has some tension.

Flux the beak area of the bird and the back of the beak, and then solder with easy solder.

Silver Bird

The silver bird has three pieces of tubing, each 4 mm long, soldered on the back of the tail feather area. Ball up three 4-inch-long (10.2 cm) half-hard wires, and apply a liver of sulphur patina. String the beads, thread the wire through the tubing, and make a hook. Use a touch of glue to keep the wires from swiveling.

Apply a liver of sulphur patina on the bird and, using the photo as a guide, pumice around the middle, leaving the edges darkened.

The wing has two holes drilled in it with a #65 drill bit. Remember to drill first with a small drill bit and work your way up. Color the copper wing with hobby or model car spray paint. This particular wing was painted, then sanded and painted again for texture. Connect the wing with a staple rivet using 20-gauge wire.

Brass Bird

The brass bird has three 20-gauge wires, each 5 inches (12.7 cm) long soldered to the back tail feather area.

The surface of the bird was created by a happy accident when I let the bird sit in the pickle too long accompanied by a few copper pieces. I sanded away some of the copper-plated areas and then used a low heat patina to color it.

Connect the silver wing to the bird using the brass nuts and bolts. Slide the bolt through from the front side of the wing and bird. String a washer, and then screw the nut down so it's snug. Saw the excess bolt away, leaving about a millimeter. Deburr, and hammer with the round end of the chasing hammer—creating a rivet to keep the nut from coming off.

String the desired beads onto the wires, and finish the ends with a spiral. If you'd like, you can hammer the spirals.

spiral tag set

I find spiral design punches irresistible. When overlapped, they remind me of some cool tin pieces I saw on the streets of Katmandu, and that was the beginning of my inspiration.

❀

WHAT YOU NEED

EARRINGS
Toolbox (page 12)
20-gauge sterling sheet metal
Dividers
Metal cutting shears
#65 drill bit
Masking tape
Spiral stamp tool
Heavy-duty household claw hammer
22-gauge sterling wire
Torch
6 diamond-shaped garnet beads,
    5 mm
4 round garnet beads, 5 mm
20-gauge half-hard silver wire
Ring mandrel or dowel rod
10 silver jump rings, 3 mm
18 silver jump rings, 5 mm

HOW TO MAKE IT

Make the tags

Set your dividers to ⁵⁄₁₆ inches (8 mm) wide, and scribe a line down the side of your metal sheet. Cut down the scribed line with shears. Reset your dividers to ¼ inch (6 mm) wide, scribe a line on the strip, and cut. Don't worry if your cuts aren't perfectly straight. Repeat until you have 10 tags.

Center punch the top center of each tag, and drill with a #65 drill bit. Lightly sand the pieces to a 600-grit finish. The tiny pieces are tricky to hold on to while sanding, so I make a small masking tape loop for the end of my finger and stick it on that. Take care to not go crazy on the sanding because it will really thin your metal, and it's already thin to begin with.

Each tag has an overlapping stamped design. When it comes to picking a stamp, you can use letters, the end of a screwdriver, a design like this tiny spiral—anything will work. You might want to test the effect on a piece of copper first.

Place the tag on the bench block with the punch in place. Strike the punch with a heavy-duty claw hammer. Repeat, overlapping the design here and there. Like the cut edges, it's okay if some of your stamps are irregular.

File and sand the edges of each tag, rounding the corners slightly so they aren't sharp.

spiral tag set

Beaded dangles

Cut ten 1-inch (2.5 cm) pieces of 22-gauge wire, and ball up the ends. String a garnet bead onto a wire and finish with a wrapped loop. Repeat to make nine more beaded dangles.

Create the ear wires

Ball up two 2-inch (5 cm) pieces of 20-gauge half-hard silver wire. Hammer the ball if you like, and make a small hook at the balled-up end using round-nose pliers. Wrap the remaining section around a mandrel or dowel rod.

Patina

Oxidize all the parts and pieces for the earrings in liver of sulphur. Pumice each of the pieces, especially the tags so the texture pops out, then brass brush or tumble.

Assembly

Connect a 3 mm jump ring to each of the tags. Hang a tag and a 5 mm jump ring on a 5 mm jump ring and close the ring. Open another 5 mm jump ring and hang a tag, the previous ring, a garnet dangle and another 5 mm jump ring. Repeat the last step except connect the tag and round garnet dangle in reverse order. See the illustration for a layout of the components and order.

Finish by hanging the chain and last garnet dangle on the ear wire.

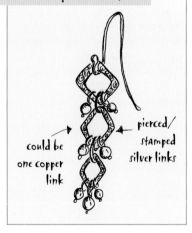

From My Sketchpad

could be one copper link

pierced/ stamped silver links

WHAT YOU NEED

RING

Toolbox (page 14)

24-gauge sterling wire

Torch

5 round garnet beads, 5 mm

5 diamond garnet beads, 5 mm

Steel ring mandrel and vise

Sterling ring band, 5 mm width

Spiral decorative stamp

Heavy-duty hammer

Wooden dowel

#55 drill bit

18-gauge half-hard wire

Third hand tool

Flux

Sterling bead cap, 8.7 mm

Easy solder

HOW TO MAKE IT

Beaded dangles

Cut ten 1-inch (2.5 cm) wires, and ball up the ends. String a garnet onto each wire and finish with a wrapped loop.

Make the ring

Put the steel ring mandrel in a vise. Slide the ring on the mandrel and texture with the spiral stamp, overlapping the design.

With the ring on the mandrel, center punch the middle of the ring band. Remove the ring, and insert a wooden dowel rod for support while you drill.

Cut a 1-inch (2.5 cm) piece of 18-gauge half-hard wire, and thread it through the hole. Hold the end of the wire inside the ring with the third hand tool. Flux the top of the ring and backside of the bead cap. Slide the bead cap over the wire so it sits centered on top of the ring. Place chips of solder next to the bead cap's hole and wire, and then solder. Draw the solder around the bead cap and down through the hole in the ring. Pickle and check the join.

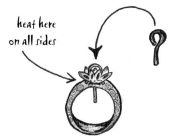

heat here
on all sides

Trim the excess wire from inside the ring. Cut the top wire so it's approximately ⅜ inch (9.5 mm) long, and make a loop. Sand the inside of the ring so there's no trace of the wire.

Put the beaded dangles and ring piece into liver of sulphur. Pumice away the high spots, and brass brush.

Connect the dangles

Open the loop and connect the 10 dangles, alternating between diamond and round garnets.

graceful "S" clasp

Multi-strand necklaces are striking and this clasp makes it easy to interchange the strands. You can wear one chunky strand or half a dozen small strands and still use the same clasp.

WHAT YOU NEED

- Toolbox (page 12)
- 12-gauge round silver wire
- Ring mandrel and vise
- Riveting hammer
- Wood block (optional)
- 20-gauge copper wire
- 49-strand nylon-coated beading wire, .018 diameter
- 3 strands of focal beads
- Metal spacer beads
- Scrimp closure findings
- Soldered jump rings, 6 mm

HOW TO MAKE IT

Making the S

It's worth mentioning how hard it is to bend the end of this thick 12-gauge wire by hand. Measuring in 2 to 3 inches (5 to 7.6 cm) to begin your first curve makes things a little easier and gives you some leverage. You'll have to cut the excess wire off, but you can always make a toggle bar with it later.

Put the ring mandrel in a vise and wrap the wire around it, making almost a full circle. The openings in the "S" shown here are approximately ⅝ inch (1.6 cm). Reposition the piece so that the loop is at the top of the mandrel and the remaining wire is off to one side. Bring the wire down and back up the other side of the mandrel. At this point it may look more like an "8" than an "S."

Cut off the extra wire to create the "S" form. Round out the ends of the wire with a file and some sanding.

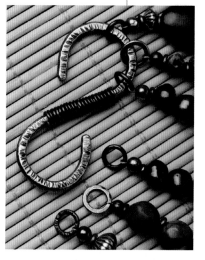

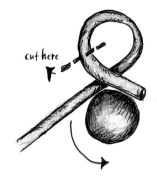

cut here

graceful 'S' clasp

Hammer the "S" to make your desired texture. I textured both sides with different hammers to add some variety. If you take this route, don't place the "S" on the steel block for the second side, but instead rest it on a wood block. This is a softer surface and won't flatten the first side's texture.

Wrap the center section of the "S" with 20-gauge copper wire. Oxidize the piece with liver of sulphur, and pumice away the oxidation on the high spots. Finish with a brass brush or by tumbling.

Beading
This is a fun clasp for either a single strand or multiple strands of beads. Try one big strand of chunky beads, three same length strands of beads twisted together, or three graduated strands (16, 17, and 19 inches [40.6, 43.2, and 48.3 cm]), as seen in the project photo.

The strands are crimped to ¼- to ⁵⁄₁₆-inch (6 to 8 mm) jump rings made from soldered copper or fused silver. Texture the jump rings by sliding them on a mandrel and hammering or stamping them.

More Ideas

Variation
I really love all the swirly and curly fonts available in word processing programs. So for a different look, find a font you like and type "S." Enlarge it to the desired size, cut it out, glue it to the silver sheet, and saw it out. EASY! File and sand as usual and then, if you want, texture it using 150-grit sandpaper in a circular motion. This "S" was also domed in a hardwood dapping block.

Beaded Chain
A really easy way to add interest to a chain is by wrapping the beaded link with a different gauge wire. Make the link with 20-gauge wire and then wrap it with 22-gauge or 24-gauge wire.

organic techno bangle

Drill anything from rocks to beach glass to create intriguing beads. The sleek metal emphasizes and enhances the organic components.

organic techno bangle

Toolbox (page 12)
12-gauge silver wire
#65 drill bit
Round mandrel (optional)
20-gauge sterling wire
Beads with large holes
Pickle
Various gauge sterling or gold-
    filled wires

Make the bangle (top bangle shown in photo below)

When I created this bangle, I wasn't sure how big to make it because there has to be some space allowance for those fun, chunky beads. Start by finding a bangle that you like from your jewelry collection and measuring the diameter. Add 1 to 1½ inches (2.5 to 3.8 cm) to your measurement, and cut the 12-gauge silver wire to that length. Lay the end of the wire on a steel surface and hammer with the flat side of a chasing hammer to flare the end (you might want some earplugs). Center punch the center of the flared end, and drill a hole with the #65 bit. Wrap the wire around a round form such as a steel bracelet mandrel so the ends overlap. I only have an oval mandrel so I actually used the round leg of my worktable. If you'd like, you can hammer the length of the wire to add some subtle texture.

String the beads on the bracelet and check the fit. Adjust the diameter of the bangle if needed. Flare and drill the remaining end of the wire.

Cut two 3½-inch (8.9 cm) pieces of 20-gauge wire, and ball up the ends. Pickle the wires and clean them as usual. Double check the bangle size, thread one end of the wire through the front side of the bracelet, and wrap around the two pieces of wire. Repeat for the opposite side.

Smaller coils of wire in various lengths and gauges can be wrapped around the bracelet.

Finish by dipping the piece in a liver of sulphur solution. Pumice the high points, and brass brush or tumble.

Variation note

The ends of wire overlap and are secured with two pieces of crimped tubing with wrapped gold wire in the middle.

Tip

You can make beads out of stones or beach glass or enlarge existing holes using diamond burrs. Attach the appropriate diamond burr to your flex shaft, and set up your work area so it can get a little messy—a layer of newsprint or plastic works nicely. You'll also need a small bowl of water to dip the stone in between drillings. This keeps the bit cool and rinses away the sludge.

leafy lariat

You can use any shape for a lariat necklace. This one was nature inspired, but geometric or abstract organic shapes would work great, too. You could also create a beaded strand instead of a chain—all interchangeable of course.

✳

WHAT YOU NEED

Toolbox (page 12)

Pattern (page 126)

18-gauge sterling sheet metal,
    2 x 1¾ inches (5 x 4.4 cm)

#55 drill bit

Doming block and punch set

2¾-inch (7 cm) length of 12-gauge
    sterling silver wire

Ring mandrel

Easy solder

Flux

Torch

Third hand tool

Fire block

9 amber faceted beads, 9 x 7 mm

20-gauge sterling half-hard wire

13-inch (33 cm) length of sterling
    silver chain, 7 mm links

10 gunmetal colored head pins,
    2 inches (5 cm) long

3 light yellow faceted beads, 8 x 5 mm

3 rust red freshwater pearls, 5 mm

3 tan faceted beads, 8 x 5 mm

2 wood beads, 4 mm

2 rectangular bronze cube beads,
    8 x 5 mm

2 amber glass round beads, 5 mm

HOW TO MAKE IT

Create the leaf

Transfer the leaf template to the 18-gauge sheet metal, and saw it out. Center punch and drill a hole in the center of the leaf. Pierce out the center shape. File and sand the leaf to a 600-grit finish.

Lay the leaf on the steel bench block, and texture it with the round end of the chasing hammer. Dome the piece in the wood doming block to give it a little depth.

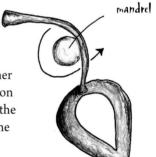

mandrel

Wrap the 12-gauge wire around the ring mandrel so there is an approximate ⅜-inch (9.5 mm) opening. One end of the wire should end up at 3 o'clock and the other at 6. Lay the 3 o'clock end of the wire on the bench block, and hammer it with the flat face of the chasing hammer. File the ends so there are no sharp edges.

Flux the wire and leaf where they'll be joined, and solder using easy solder. It helps to clip the wire in the third hand tool and then put the leaf in place on the fire block. Pickle and clean the leaf piece.

leafy lariat

Assemble the chain links

String one amber bead on the sterling half-hard wire, and finish the end with a loop. Slide the bead up next to the loop, trim the wire, and finish with another loop. Position the loops so they are perpendicular to each other using the flat-nose pliers. Repeat five more times.

Cut the chain into six 1½-inch (3.8 cm) pieces and one 3½-inch (8.9 cm) piece. Connect each of the shorter chain pieces together using the amber bead links, and then add the longer piece to one end.

Patina

Oxidize the leaf and chain pieces in liver of sulphur. Pumice the high spots on everything, but leave the stem black. Brass brush the chain and leaf.

Making the toggle

Connect the short section of chain to the end of the leaf. String two beads on each of the 10 gunmetal head pins, and attach these to the end of the 3½-inch (8.9 cm) section of chain.

From My Sketchpad

nylon chain instead of metal (it's easy to swap out chains)

beaded with chain

holes for more dangles

under the sea

The inspiration for this piece came from the glass focal bead. To me, it looked like something you might see in the ocean surrounded by coral, so it felt right to include the red coral accents.

under the sea

WHAT YOU NEED

Toolbox (page 12)
Aqua glass beads, 12 mm
20-gauge wire coil
Dyed coral beads, 5 to 20 mm
22-gauge fine silver wire
Bezel mandrel
18-gauge fine silver wire
Ring mandrel
Scribe
Rubber tubing, (optional,
    if needed)
Glass focal pendant, 32 mm
20-gauge sterling sheet metal
#65 drill bit
Dapping block and punch set
20-gauge sterling half-hard wire
Torch
11 silver jump rings, 5 mm

HOW TO MAKE IT

Making bead links

String an aqua bead onto the 20-gauge wire coil, and make a loop at the end. Slide the bead up against the loop, and make a 90° bend. Trim the wire, and make another loop to create a beaded link. Position the loops so they're perpendicular to each other. Repeat four more times with aqua beads and five more times using two coral beads.

Making the loop and loop chain

Using the 22-gauge fine silver wire, follow the instructions in the Basic section for how to make a jump ring. You only need 40 rings, but I usually make about 10 extra in case one pulls apart or doesn't fuse nicely. Make sure the ends of each ring fit together snugly, and fuse them together. Push the rings onto the bezel mandrel to make them perfectly circular.

Refer to the Making a Loop-in-Loop Chain sidebar on page 37, and make 40 links.

Thread one loop piece through the loop on the next, and repeat two more times for a total of four links per chain section. Eight regular sections are needed to create the necklace. One dangle has the loop-in-loop chain started on a small teardrop link.

Large tear links

Cut five 1½-inch (3.8 cm) lengths of 18-gauge fine silver wire; four 2-inch (5 cm) lengths; and one 2¼-inch (5.7 cm) length. Fuse the ends of the wires together, and push them over the ring mandrel to round them out.

Slide a ring on the bezel mandrel, and insert a scribe into the ring as well. Pull the two apart so it creates a large rounded side and a sharp angle. You can adjust the curve by sliding it up or down the mandrel and pulling again.

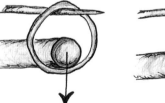

Wire pinch bail

Create a pinch bail for the coral to dangle from by making a wire triangle. Slide the two ends into a coral bead and pinch closed.

Prepping the focal pendant

Lay the circle template over the front of the pendant and choose a circle size for your bead cap; repeat for the backside. Scribe the circles on the 20-gauge silver sheet, saw them out, and sand the edges. Drill a hole in the center of the front disc with a #65 drill bit, and slightly dome it to fit the front of the pendant. Leave the back circle piece flat. Essentially, we're making a "sandwich" for the bead.

Make a spiral at the end of the 20-gauge wire and run it through the bead cap, focal bead, and back bead cap. Finish the end with a hook-like shape.

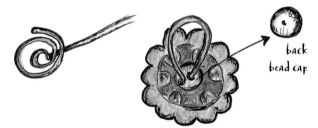

back bead cap

Toggle clasp

Cut a 1¼-inch (3.2 cm) length of the 20-gauge half-hard sterling wire, and ball it up. Place the middle of the wire over the end of the bezel mandrel and make one full wrap. Hammer on both sides of the loop to flatten.

Note

If the hole through your pendant is too large, you can run a piece of tubing through it to lessen the hole size.

Connect it all together

Put all the silver pieces in liver of sulphur, and then pumice away the high spots. Brass brush all the pieces.

Hang two sections of chain (one being the small teardrop linked in) on the 20-gauge hook that's on the backside of the pendant. Connect a coral dangle to both ends of the chain.

You'll note that the order of chain and links is a tad random. Refer to the photo as a guide for the order. Use jump rings to connect the sections of chain to the bead or teardrop links and toggle clasp ends.

wild
vines

This multi-strand finding came about when I wanted to create something that could have multiple uses, such as a chandelier earring or a pendant.

✦

WHAT YOU NEED

Toolbox (page 12)

Pattern (page 126)

20-gauge sterling sheet metal

16-gauge fine silver wire

Torch

Flux

Easy solder

18-gauge silver wire

#65 drill bit

49 strand nylon coated beading wire, .018 diameter

14 scrimp findings

82 black glass pearls, 4 mm

16 burgundy freshwater pearls, 4 mm

42 blue/purple glass beads, 4 mm

12 purple beads (drilled off center)

Matte gray Delica seed beads

39 burgundy freshwater pearls, 6 mm

10 inch (25.4 cm) length of sterling silver chain, 10mm links

4 silver jump rings, 6 mm

HOW TO MAKE IT

Make the findings

Transfer the leaf multi-strand finding and clasp patterns to the sheet metal and saw them out. Drill the holes in each of the leaf multi-strand findings using a #65 bit. File the edges and sand to a 600-grit finish.

Use a center punch and mallet to create a dotted texture on the leaf clasp and on the outside leaves of the multi-strand finding.

Make two ⅞-inch-diameter (2.2 cm) rings with the 16-gauge wire and then fuse them. Hammer the rings with the flat side of a chasing hammer on a steel bench block.

Flux the areas where the pieces will be joined. For the multi-strand finding, lay the single leaf face down on the solder block. Lay the second piece face down on the center leaf and align. The piece may tip to one side so slide an 18-gauge wire under the rounded side of the finding. Place a chip of easy solder next to the joint and heat. When the solder begins to flow, draw it to the opposite side of the connector bar. Quench and pickle.

This wire props the ring up so it lays flat against the single leaf to make a good join

🔳 = solder chip

wild vines

To make the clasp, align the rounded part of the leaf with the ring, stem facing outward, and solder as you did before. Quench and pickle. Twirl the stem under using round-nose pliers to make a hook for the clasp.

Oxidize the components with liver of sulphur and pumice the surfaces except for the center leaves on the multi-strand findings. Brass brush or tumble.

Beading
The strands connected to the leaves with scrimp findings are strung in this order: black pearl, freshwater pearl , black pearl, purple/blue bead, purple bead, and blue purple bead. Using the project photo as a guide, repeat this sequence for each of the rows.

The beaded strands on the sides are connected to the rings with seed bead loops using the grey Delicas and scrimp findings. The outer strand alternates between black glass and 6 mm freshwater pearls. The middle strand is a 5-inch (12.7 cm) section of silver chain that has been oxidized, pumiced and polished, and connected with jump rings. The inside strand is strung in this order: black pearl, purple/blue bead, black pearl, then a 4 mm burgundy freshwater pearl.

From My Sketchpad

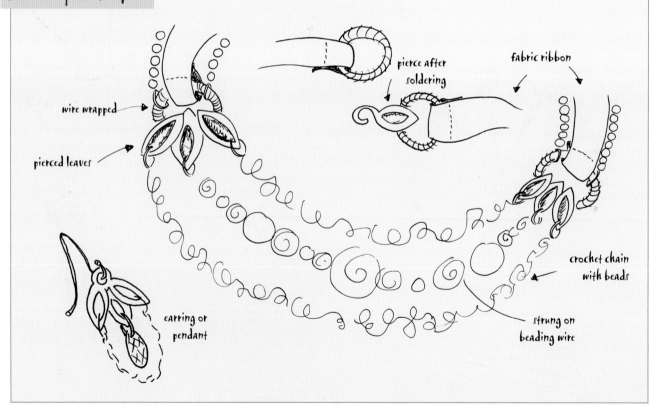

wire wrapped

pierced leaves

pierce after soldering

fabric ribbon

earring or pendant

crochet chain with beads

strung on beading wire

patterns
(actual size)

Gingko Necklace

Fanciful Feathered Friend

Serene Cross

Fiesta Flower

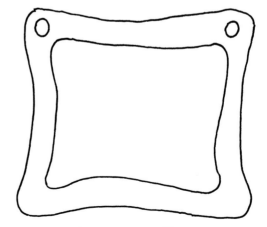

Woven Copper Necklace

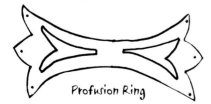

Profusion Ring

templates

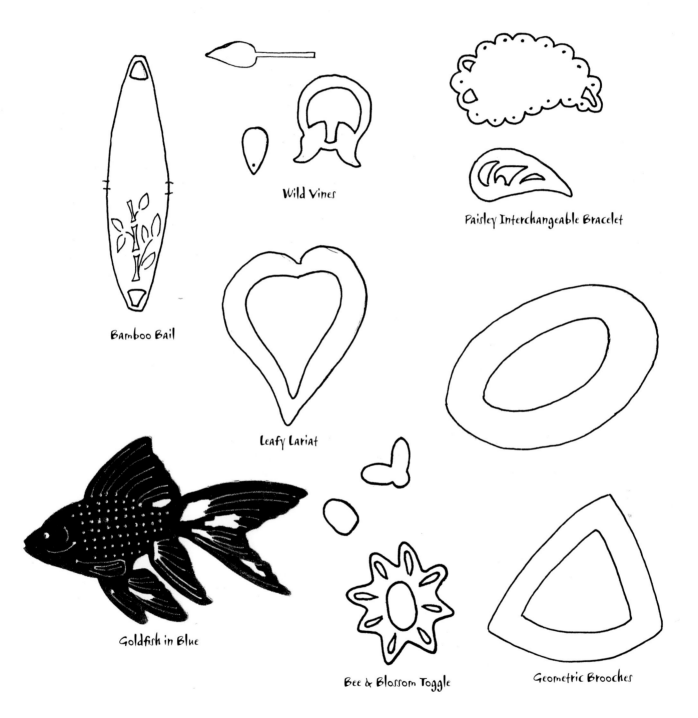

Bamboo Bail

Wild Vines

Paisley Interchangeable Bracelet

Leafy Lariat

Goldfish in Blue

Bee & Blossom Toggle

Geometric Brooches

acknowledgments

Thank you to everyone at Lark Books and Sterling Publishing. It is truly a privilege to be one of your authors.

To my editor, Linda Kopp, you are a saint. Words can't express my gratitude for your energy and support every step of the way. You are truly a friend, and I hope we have many more adventures together.

A warm thank you to Kathy Holmes, art director and a fellow Hoosier! Thank you for making the pages of this book stunning. And for believing I could do my own illustrations!

Thank you, Lynne Harty, for the absolutely gorgeous photography in this book. My pieces look so beautiful because of you.

To Marthe LeVan, Terry Taylor, Nicole McConville, Amanda Carestio—from acquisitions to proofing photos and text, thank you for everything you do to help make a book come to life.

Big hugs to my friends, Katie Hacker, Mary Hettmansperger, and Cynthia Deis. Thank you always for your words of wisdom and encouragement. Each of you has written a book (or several) and know what I'm talking about. And Katie, a special thank you for the beading day that went into the night. What a friend you are!

To my family, thank you for all your love and support. I am so lucky to be able to call you my family.

To Robin Kraft, my college metalsmithing professor, you were always so generous with your time. Thank you for everything you taught me in class and outside of class.

To the fabulous art bead makers, you are one of the reasons this book was written. Thank you to the talented Cindy Gimbrone, Heather Powers, Stephanie Sersich, Jennifer Heynen, and Melanie Brooks Lukacs.

To the awesome companies who supplied fabulous materials for this book, thank you Fire Mountain Gems, Beadalon, Beaducation, Bead Trust, Ornamentea, and Clover Needlecrafts.

about the author

Candie Cooper is a jewelry designer with a passion for combining unique materials and color combinations, inspired by extensive travel and her years living in China. Candie is the author of *Felted Jewelry* (Lark Books 2007) and *Designer Needle Felting* (Lark Books 2007) and is a contributing designer in Lark's *Fabulous Found Object Jewelry, Beading with Crystals,* and *Beading with Charms.* Currently she's creating designs for a variety of companies in the craft industry as well as for craft and jewelry-making publications. Candie teaches workshops both nationally and internationally and has appeared on the Public Television series *Beads, Baubles, and Jewels.* She earned a Bachelor's degree in Art Education and Fine Arts from Purdue University. For further information, please visit www.candiecooper.com.

index